Completing the Circle

the Circle

Reviewing Ministries in the Congregation

DAVID R. MCMAHILL

FOREWORD BY
CLYDE J. STECKEL

D1316584

THE
ALBAN
INSTITUTE

www.alban.org

Library of Congress Catalog Card Number 2002116299
ISBN 1-56699-278-8

Contents

Foreword

I looked for just this book during all my 30-plus years of seminary teaching in the field of the practice of ministry. Why this book? Because early in my ministry, which included parish ministry, hospital chaplaincy, and campus ministry, I became persuaded that performance evaluations of clergy were going on all the time, but they were, for the most part, informal and unacknowledged. Thriving in the kind of gossip network that exists in every church, these informal evaluations could be favorable if the numbers moved upward. When church membership, pledging and giving, program development, staff hiring, and building programs grew, evaluations of clergy were generally positive. Furthermore, if the minister preached good sermons, was a friendly, outgoing person, and visited faithfully in homes and hospitals, so much the better. But if some part of that picture was missing, members quickly concluded there must be something wrong with the minister's leadership.

As a seminary teacher in the practical field, I explored theoretical models and procedures for performance reviews from institutions where such reviews are a matter of course—business; government; schools, colleges, and universities; health care institutions; arts and cultural institutions; and the like. I believed then, and still believe, that the church could learn much from such institutions and their performance evaluations. I believed that a shared, open, principled set of evaluative procedures would protect both the clergy and the church from the pain and destruction often inflicted when informal and unacknowledged evaluations run amok.

But something essential was missing in these models borrowed from other institutions. It was not just the inappropriateness of evaluating ministerial leadership primarily by refering to the balance sheet. Even in human service institutions, where gains and losses cannot be so readily quantified, evaluating leadership performance was properly understood to be a matter of employer–employee contractual obligations. Slowly I realized that none of these models worked for the church, where the calling or appointing of pastoral leadership is a matter of spiritual discernment, a covenant involving not just the church and the pastor, but the very Spirit of the living God known in Jesus Christ.

In this wonderful new book, *Completing the Circle: Reviewing Ministries in the Congregation,* David McMahill offers both a model and a procedure for clergy performance evaluation that is spiritually grounded and theologically explicated in just the right way. He makes it clear that performance evaluation should be an ongoing and normative experience in the life of the congregation—thus, over time, diminishing the fear that evaluation is always a negative experience, or that evaluation only happens when something is wrong. And McMahill makes it clear that it is the purpose and mission of the church—not just the likes and dislikes of the people regarding a particular minister—that finally grounds any proper performance evaluation.

Three particular strengths of this book are the author's warnings about consumerism in the church; his detailed methodology for ensuring that evaluative information is high quality, useful, and appropriate; and his emphasis on healthy interpersonal communication in a local church system.

Consumerism—the belief that any enterprise is finally to be judged by whether its goods and services are satisfying to the consumer—is one of the blights of our time. As a voluntary institution, the church strives to maintain an often precarious balance between satisfying and challenging people. If all a church's members (the consumers) are happy with everything the church provides for them, if there is no challenge, if people are not stirred up, then something is terribly wrong. Perhaps it is not just consumerism, but also the individualism of our time, the unrealistic expectation that each person can fully achieve, indeed *deserves* to reach, his or her personal goals. The church has a message about God's gracious love for such seekers, but it may not always strike them as what they want.

Clearly a major strength of *Completing the Circle* is the precise techniques McMahill offers for eliciting the kind of high quality feedback a church needs to engage in performance evaluation. By "high quality feedback," McMahill means observations framed in the experience of participants—experiences, not evaluations. These gathered experiences eventually do lead to evaluations, but they must be framed experientially. A person must say that "my experience of listening to the pastor's sermons is such and such," not "Those are bad (or good) sermons." This will require rigorous discipline on the part of those leading the evaluative process, something that may take some time to learn, especially in a church culture where everyone is constantly judging everything about the lay or pastoral leaders. But if a church will learn and practice McMahill's method with disciplined care, great benefits will follow for the church and the pastor.

Beneath this way of gathering useful feedback lie those principles for healthy communication common to all human settings. McMahill is both clear and persuasive on these principles. While he does not fully explain what to do when people choose to ignore sound interpersonal principles and act in less than healthy ways, the many examples he gives will point the way. Leaders must not respond in kind, but must continue to practice healthy communication even in the face of such subversion. That may slow things down, but it will not ultimately defeat the process.

This book deserves wide readership, but more than that, even wider application. Both churches and clergy will profit immensely from its use.

Clyde J. Steckel
Emeritus Professor of Theology
United Theological Seminary of the Twin Cities

Preface

Questions and Foundations

I have been a United Church of Christ minister since 1970, and have been the Eastern Association minister in the Minnesota Conference, United Church of Christ, since 1995. In this position, I serve as pastor to pastors for the more than 260 UCC clergy who hold ministerial standing in the Eastern Association. I am often the first person to be called by members of association churches searching for resources from the wider church.

On my second day on the job in 1995, I received three phone calls from laypeople looking for resources on "how to evaluate our minister." I was hesitant to suggest any of the material on pastoral evaluation I had seen. I knew of several churches in which a poorly constructed process for evaluating ministers had spun out of control, morphing into a power struggle between congregational factions as to whose ideas about the church and its ministry would prevail.

Having recently read Roy Oswald's *Getting a Fix on Your Ministry: A Practical Guide to Clergy Performance Appraisal,* I took to heart his strong cautions about generic performance evaluations for clergy.[1] I agree that it is probably better that a church not attempt an evaluation process at all than do one carelessly or use a process that does not take into account the specific congregation or the unique covenantal relationship between minister and congregation. I asked each of the callers what the congregation wanted to accomplish with a formal evaluation of its minister. The first caller said he understood that conducting an evaluation was just a good, businesslike thing to do. He himself worked for a local government that had annual performance evaluations. The second caller said she was hoping that an evaluation would persuade her minister to change some annoying behaviors. "Either he changes or he should leave. Maybe it's too late for change to do any good." The third caller said that his congregation argued every year when the time came to vote on a recommended salary increase for the minister. "If we have the results of an evaluation," he said, "then we have something concrete to show people as a reason for either giving, or not giving, a salary increase."

Each caller wanted an evaluation form that could be mailed to church members, polling their opinions on various aspects of the minister's work. I am sure I disappointed them by saying that I knew of no such form that I could recommend wholeheartedly. I told them I would keep watching and would let them know when I found something workable and appropriate.

The next day, I received another call, the first of many along these lines: "Reverend McMahill, I'm not an officer of my church but just a concerned lay member. I don't know what we are going to do about our minister. People are leaving the church in droves. Most of the confirmation class has quit coming. His sermons are rambling and show no preparation. I think he just makes them up on the spot! Our offerings are way down. You've got to come right away and intervene before this place just explodes."

"My gracious," I said. "This sounds serious. Have you talked with your minister about these concerns? What does he say about them?"

"I tried, but he just wrote me off and said that as far as he knows, there is nothing wrong. Well, 'nothing that couldn't be fixed by a few strategic funerals,' is how he put it. I wonder if he thought I was one of those he was wishing would die. I won't give him the satisfaction of doing my funeral, believe me!"

"Hm, well, have you tried talking to the church officers, or do you have a parish-pastor relations committee or something like that?" I asked. "Or have you told the moderator or the deacons that you have some big concerns?"

"Actually, no, because I don't think that would do any good. Our minister has all those people in his hip pocket, and they do whatever he tells them. Whatever he wants, that's what they do," she said.

"Getting back to your talking directly to your minister, can you tell me what it was like when you last talked with him about your concerns?" I asked.

"Well, see, I'm not very good at this sort of thing, so I'm not sure I got my point across. I hate confrontation. I'd rather tell you and have you tell our minister that we are ready for him to move on. That's your job, isn't it?" she said.

"No, it isn't my job. Besides, if I were in your minister's shoes, and my association minister called and said that someone was really upset with me, I would want to know who and why and what the concerns were," I said. "It is always far better for people who are upset to go directly to the minister and lay it all out. So are you saying you did or did not tell your minister about your concerns?"

"I sort of did, but I guess I toned it down. I am just really afraid he'll yell at me or take it out on me some other way," she replied.

"I know in some churches the parish-pastor relations committee will try to help members and the minister talk to each other if people are having a hard time with that. Does yours do anything like that?" I asked.

"Look," she said, "I don't even know who is on it, or if they are even meeting. I have never heard of anyone ever even trying to take anything to that committee, if it even exists. See, I called you because I assumed you would be able to see to it that our minister gets placed somewhere else, and then you would get us someone better suited for our needs."

I replied, "In our system I don't and can't do that. When a minister moves, of course, I come to help your church search for a new minister, but I don't move people or place them. What I can do is to meet with your lay leaders and your minister to figure out how to talk about these concerns and to try to find some solutions. So as a first step, I need to let your minister know about this call. Then we'll try to find a way to look at these issues and deal with them."

There was a long pause. "Would you have to use my name?" she asked.

I said, "If you were the minister, what would you like?"

She said, "I would want to know who was mad at me and why. Oh, my. I'm not very anxious for you to use my name, but do what you have to do." Then she hung up.

Uh-oh, I thought. An angry church, maybe. At least one angry member, for sure, and maybe more—maybe for good reason, and maybe not. But if this caller is accurate, the minister doesn't seem to know about the unrest she described. Is good feedback getting to the minister? Is good feedback getting to the lay leaders? Doesn't sound like it—but who knows? If systems are in place for giving reliable feedback to the minister and the lay leaders, this church member either doesn't know about those systems or doesn't trust them. Could it be that she isn't really interested in giving good feedback but would rather wallow in her unhappiness? Could it be that the minister is sending subtle but clear messages of disrespect toward women? Or could it be that the caller has had so many bad experiences with men that she is projecting all of her past anger toward men onto her minister? Clearly, something was terribly wrong here; but without better information, I had no idea how to be helpful.

My mind flashed back to a discussion in one of my seminary classes with Dr. Ross Snyder at Chicago Theological Seminary. Ross Snyder was a great teacher and advocate of effective, healthy interpersonal communication. One day after leading our class through an exercise on "active listening," Snyder made what I am sure was meant to be a throwaway comment, "The sermon is a terrible example of effective interpersonal communication. In fact, that's true of most of our typical church life." I remember thinking, "Wait a minute. Why? Why can't we do better than that?" At the time, I didn't have an abundance of good ideas, but the question stayed with me. The complaint I had just received from that angry church member seemed to confirm what Snyder had said years ago. If that congregation had managed to create a culture of healthy communication, some members might still be angry, but at least they would know where to take their anger.

Healthy interpersonal communication has been for me a strong interest and a high value as long as I can remember. In my high school years, I was nurtured by various leadership training programs offered through the YMCA, especially Hi-Y (High School YMCA). I still remember the evening when one of our advisors led our Hi-Y group through a learning experience on the "circle of communication." Our advisor, Ralph Wood, of the Omaha YMCA, gave one of our members an abstract drawing composed of about a dozen geometric figures hooked together. Everyone else had a blank sheet of paper. The person with the drawing was told to describe the drawing as carefully as possible. The goal was for the rest of us to draw something resembling the drawing on the leader's paper. We were given only two rules. One, we could not compare results with each other, and, two, we could not ask questions of the leader.

The leader described the drawing on her paper carefully and in minute detail, but despite her efforts, none of us came close to producing a drawing that looked like hers.

Then another leader was chosen and given a different drawing. The assignment was the same, except that this time we could compare our efforts and ask as many questions as we liked. To no one's surprise, when we compared what we had drawn to the design the leader had described, all of us had a nearly perfect match. Several were a bit off in size, but we all had the right figures correctly placed and shaped.

What we experienced in that exercise was the importance of feedback in completing the circle of communication. Now, more than 35 years later, I don't remember clearly how much more was said that night about the importance of feedback in the circle of communication, but the experience prompted a great deal of my own thinking about communication. I have used that exercise in training workshops for leaders of congregations. It helps make the point that interpersonal communication begins with a message in the mind of the sender. That message is conveyed with words, vocal inflections, and body language. Much can happen to that message before it is received, and several tries may be needed before the *received* message is the same as the *intended* message. That's why feedback is essential. Feedback may be offered in the form of a question: "Did you mean a, b, and c?" Feedback may be given as a statement, "I hear you saying, x, y, and z." Feedback may also include an exchange among multiple hearers of the original message: "This is what I heard. Is that what you heard?" Feedback may be given as a response from the receiver to the sender that says, "This is how I react to what you have done [or said]." Feedback allows the original sender to clarify the message he or she intended to communicate and to confirm its arrival when the receivers have apparently heard the message that was intended.

The health of any human organization depends greatly on how effectively its members communicate. If systems and habits of reliable feedback are in place, the organization can usually find a way to solve most problems that confront it. But if these systems and habits are not in place, the organization will tend to be run by those who have power (or who want it), and it will eventually disintegrate and die. Thus, one crucial task of leadership is to ensure that effective systems of communication—which require reliable feedback—are put in place and become part of the habit of the organization.

As I thought about the needs of that church whose angry member had called, another experience came to mind. The board of deacons at a church my wife and I once served (we were co-pastors) was struggling with a decision about Holy Communion. In the United Church of Christ, the manner of receiving the communion elements is a local church decision. Some congregations distribute little pieces of bread (or wafers or rice cakes) and little cups of juice (or wine, or, in one church I know of, grape Kool-Aid!) to worshipers in the pews. Other congregations invite worshipers to come forward, break off a piece of bread from a common loaf, and dip it in a chalice with either juice or wine. (This method is called "intinction.") Some churches do a combination of all this and more.

Many congregations are sensitive about changing their manner of celebrating communion. Although change is not impossible, a compelling reason to change had better be presented. In the church we were serving, the long-standing custom was to serve worshipers in the pews. Then a large construction project took the kitchen out of commission for a while. Suddenly the task of washing several hundred little communion cups became a big problem. The deacons announced to the congregation, "For the duration of the construction, we will observe communion by intinction because it is so much easier to wash one chalice in a bathroom sink than 200 little glasses. But as soon as construction is done, we will go back to pew communion."

The congregation was happy to cooperate, so long as the change was understood to be temporary. The deacons who assisted at the communion stations discovered something unexpected: their own response to the power of serving communion by intinction. When their church friends came forward, the deacons looked each in the eye and said, "Mary, the Body of Christ, broken for you. . . . Fred, the cup of the New Covenant, shed for you. . . ."

"Wow," said one deacon. "What an incredible experience. I don't want to go back to pew communion!" Others agreed.

"But we promised," said another. "We can't go back on our word just because we have changed our minds." Even those who said they now liked intinction acknowledged that they had made a promise.

After long discussions about how to make this decision, one deacon said, "Why don't we invite some of our church members to come to a meeting and tell us what they experience when they take communion? Let's have some tell us about receiving pew communion, and others tell us about receiving it by intinction. Some people, of course, will tell us about their experience with both styles."

That is what they did, and these conversations were astonishingly powerful. Some people spoke of their heightened sense of the community of the church when they received pew communion and the congregation was invited to partake together. Others spoke of the sense of transcendence they felt, coming forward and hearing their names spoken as they received the elements. One man spoke about the taste of the elements: "When I taste the sweet juice, I am reminded each time how good it is to eat and drink, and how good it is that God came to us in a human being who tasted, who ate and drank just as we do." Another worshiper said, "When I taste the bread and then the juice, the phrase almost always comes to my mind, 'Taste and see that the Holy One is good!'

The power of this conversation was that people heard each other—and the deacons received reliable feedback upon which to base their decisions about worship life.

As I thought about this experience and about the need to devise systems and habits comes when people report on their firsthand experiences. By "experiences," I mean what happens *to* us or what we cause to happen (that is, what might be observed by someone else) and what happens *in* us (that is, in our thoughts and feelings known only to us until we reveal them to others). As I will explain in more detail later, when we talk about our experiences, all we can ever do is to talk about our interpretation of what we think happened.

By keeping an ear to the ground, alert pastors are able to gather quite a bit of reliable, descriptive feedback. But, I wondered, what would happen if a church were to adopt practices of formally asking for descriptive feedback from church members about what they had been experiencing in the life of the church? What if the kinds of experiences we had shared about the experience of Holy Communion could be replicated in feedback about the endless numbers of other experiences we have in the life and mission of the congregation? What would that practice mean for the sense of community? How would it affect the work of those in leadership to hear regularly from people describing what they experience in their heart of hearts in various places and times in congregational life? Also, how would it affect members carrying out their ministries in the congregation and in daily life if they were given the opportunity to describe their experience and to hear others talk about theirs? And how would it affect all these folk if they had the sense that they were really "heard"? Being able to speak is great, but feeling heard is even better. Wouldn't putting in place and following a simple system of asking for descriptive feedback lead to a way to review the ministries of a local church that would be far superior to most of our current methods?

Goals for This Book

With these questions in mind, I set out to put together a model for how church leaders might ask for, receive, and make use of reliable feedback—honest feedback that people would provide about what they experience in the life of their congregation. I have shared earlier versions of this work in workshops across the Eastern Association of the Minnesota Conference of the United Church of Christ and have received dozens of excellent suggestions from participants. Many of these suggestions have been incorporated into this book.

While assembling this book, I have been guided by several important goals.

First, I want this material to be accessible to Mary and Joe Congregant, those wonderful saints who, because of their faithfulness to Christ and the church, have agreed to accept positions on their local church pastoral relations committee or the board of deacons, or other leadership posts. Although everything in this book is grounded in solid theory, I do not expect that readers will need an advanced degree to make sense of what I say here.

Making this material accessible has meant keeping it short. Busy people are not going to stay with a book that is longer than it needs to be. But I hope the material is not so brief that I offer the reader insufficient guidance and suggestions. I also hope readers will discover that giving and receiving reliable feedback is manageable and interesting.

One other way of making this material accessible is to show how the "Completing the Circle" process might be used in a local congregation. Rather than writing in the abstract and leaving it to readers to figure out how it might work, I describe much of the process in the context of one congregation, Sand Lake United Church of Christ. Does Sand Lake Church exist? Well—no and yes. You won't find a congregation of that name listed in official denominational yearbooks, but I hope you will see something in this congregation to remind you of your own community of faith. Most of what I say about Sand Lake UCC grows out of real experiences with real congregations—appropriately modified to avoid embarrassment to any individual.

Second, I hope this material will help bring about a culture of healthy communication in local churches. Considering the importance of healthy interpersonal communication in any human organization—especially in the organization whose mission it is to embody love, mercy, and justice—isn't it amazing that few congregations pay formal attention to systems that enhance healthy interpersonal communication? (I use the term "interpersonal" to distinguish this process from "mass" communication, such as newsletters, Web sites, radio, television, newspapers, and magazines.) Sharp pastors will develop their own strategies for getting feedback, such as showing up for a group that is the unofficial "nerve central" of the congregation, and paying careful attention to casual conversation. But such strategies tend to be informal and hit-or-miss; they may not provide enough reliable information. If only one congregation experiences the transformation in its life that can take place when people are committed to a culture of healthy communication, it will have been worth the effort to write this book.

Third, I hope that busy ministers will welcome the "Completing the Circle" process as a pleasant alternative to processes they may have previously experienced in reviews of their work. Many ministers who have undergone performance evaluations borrowed from secular institutions know the hazards of those evaluations, and do not look forward to a review process whereby lay leaders might be misled into making important decisions on the basis of unreliable information. Some ministers have experienced serious damage to their relationships with the congregations they serve— damage caused in large part by an evaluation process that went astray.

The most important aspect of this book is the discussion (mostly in chapter 3) about criteria and purpose. Why are we conducting a review of the ministries of our congregation? What ingredients of a good review will tell us what we want and need to know? These central questions should be asked before a congregation embarks on a review process, but all too often, they are overlooked.

Acknowledgments

I want to thank the several hundred people around the Eastern Association of the Minnesota Conference, United Church of Christ, who have attended workshops I have led on this topic, especially those who attended my earliest workshops when my ideas about this topic were agonizingly unrefined. Without exception, someone in every workshop had a suggestion to offer to make this process better. I am grateful for the many good ideas from workshop participants. I also greatly appreciate thoughtful suggestions from my colleagues, past and present, on the staff of the UCC's Minnesota Conference. By far, the largest number of excellent suggestions came from my editor, Beth Ann Gaede, who has a temperament for editing that I clearly do not possess. Most of all, the gentle feedback from my wife, who is also my favorite colleague in ministry, the Rev. Jane McMahill, has been a source of steady encouragement not only for this project but for most things that I do.

NOTE

1. Roy Oswald, *Getting a Fix on Your Ministry: A Practical Guide to Clergy Performance Appraisal* (Bethesda, Md.: Alban Institute, 1993, 2001).

To Review or Not to Review?

Shelly worked as director of human resources for a large information systems company in a large city in the upper Midwest. She was also chair of the personnel committee at Sand Lake United Church of Christ. She had invited me to meet with this committee to talk about whether to establish annual performance evaluations for the church staff.

"I don't see why this should be so hard," Shelly began. "In the company I work for, we do annual reviews for everyone. We hire people to do a particular job. We establish performance objectives, and we pay for performance. At the end of each year, we conduct an evaluation that basically asks two questions: Did you meet your performance objectives? How well did you meet them? If you exceeded our expectations, you might be in line for a promotion and a raise in salary. If you failed miserably, we ask first whether you had the resources to do the job. If you did, we might have a talk with you about how long you will be kept in this job. In either case, the report goes to your supervisor, who uses it to set new performance objectives, and then it gets tucked away in your personnel files, for reference when questions of salary increases, promotions, or job retention come up.

"It's all pretty straightforward," Shelly continued. "What I don't get is why it should be so hard for us to put together something like that for our church staff? Why can't we just use what is tried and true in companies like mine, change the titles of the positions to fit the church, and use it? Of course, we would have to come up with performance objectives, but that should be easy, right?"

"I'm not so sure," said Dale, a retired research chemist for a nearby state university. "When I was department chair at North Star University, I had to conduct annual performance reviews for everyone in my department, and the dean of the College of Arts and Sciences always did them for people like me, so I am familiar with how it is done in a setting like the university. But I'm not so sure it is a good idea to try to transplant into the church, lock, stock, and barrel, what we do in some other workplace. Maybe for some of our part-time lay staff it would be OK, but I'm not so sure about our ordained ministers. After all, what would we evaluate? And who would do it, and how would we know if the results meant anything at all? And what difference would it make?"

"For example," Dale continued, "suppose we wanted to evaluate our ministers' preaching. It's the one thing they do that the largest percentage of our congregation sees and hears often. Well, OK, maybe that isn't true for people who don't show up in church very often, but for most of us who are here a lot, preaching is the most visible thing we see them do. But suppose we want to find out if they are 'good' preachers. Everyone in the church has his or her idea about what constitutes a good sermon. I happen to think that both Reverend Charlie and Reverend Susan are really good preachers. They make me think; sometimes they make me squirm; they introduce me to ideas that are new to me—and I like that. But I happen to know another member of our church who thinks they are very poor preachers for *exactly* the same reasons. He is looking for comfort, something to reaffirm what is familiar, and, frankly, something that won't cause him to change any of his ideas or his behavior. If we were to fill out some form that asked about the quality of the sermons preached here, my form would rate them very high and his would rate them very low. Then what we get is an evaluation that doesn't tell us very much about the quality of the ministers' preaching but more about those who fill out the evaluation forms."

"Good point," said Mary, another committee member. "I work at a skilled-level nursing home, and when most of the people I work with come back from chapel services, they have two criteria for judging the sermon—whether they could hear it and how long it was. The louder and shorter the sermon, the higher the marks. Oh, and the sermon gets rave reviews if it had some good jokes."

"So then," said Dale, "suppose we were to do this and Charlie, but not Susan, was able to figure out how to preach sermons that maximized the high marks on his reviews, and suppose we then rewarded Charlie with a larger salary increase because he got high marks. But also suppose that Susan was the one who more consistently spoke from her understanding of the claims of the gospel on us, even if we didn't always like it—what would that do to the soul of our church and to the morale of our staff? Don't we run the risk of rewarding someone who knows how to make people feel good and penalizing someone who is actually more faithful to the gospel?"

"Or there is another thing," said Fritz, a graduate student at nearby North Star University. "I'm taking a course in 'Methods of Questionnaire Research' right now, and one thing I'm learning is that when you ask people for information with a questionnaire, you have to be sure they have the information you are asking for. When I think of my own involvement with this church, I have a fairly narrow perspective on it. I attend worship, I am on this committee, I come to some potlucks—in fact, as an impoverished grad student, I wish we had more of them—and once in a while I come to other special programs, but that's about it. As a single man, I don't attend a lot of family-oriented programs. I don't know much about the Sunday church school, and I've never gone to either of the ministers for counseling. I've never been in the hospital or in a nursing home. I have never been a shut-in—except for finals week—so if I were given a questionnaire to evaluate how our ministers are doing, for huge parts of what takes up their time, I have absolutely no firsthand knowledge or experience. All I have to go on is secondhand information, at best, and that is about as reliable as gossip! If we did a questionnaire evaluation, I'm not sure it would be any better than formalized gossip. In fact, I think it could be even more destructive because people would tend to believe the results of our questionnaire even more than they believe gossip. For some reason, people tend to think that the results of a questionnaire are the absolute *truth*, no matter how badly the questionnaire was designed."

Then Marvin spoke up. "I'm glad you are all saying this. I came to this meeting really worried about the idea of doing a performance evaluation of our ministers. I have some good friends at First Congregational UCC 30 miles down the interstate from us. They did a performance evaluation of their minister a couple of years ago, and it divided that church right down the middle. What happened was that some people who wanted to get rid of their minister managed to get on the personnel committee. They created a questionnaire that would give them all the ammunition they needed to support their cause. They got some pretty damaging results, and when they published the results for the whole world to see, a bunch of supporters of the minister cried foul. The minister's supporters brought a motion to the congregation's annual meeting to declare the results of the evaluation invalid. It was a mess, let me tell you. Now, I don't think for a second that there's anything like that going on here. Shelly, I know you really care a lot about our ministers and about our church, so I know you aren't asking us to do an evaluation for reasons like those at First Congregational. But we have to be really careful how we set up something like this, or we open ourselves to something like that happening down the road when there's a new committee. I love our church, but we have some people here who are quite capable of wanting to throw their weight around through an evaluation process. We sure don't need to give them a way to do that!"

"Good grief, friends," said Shelly. "What a bunch of wet blankets!—just kidding—But you've made me wonder whether we should leave well enough alone and not try to do anything like an evaluation of staff, at least not for our ordained ministers. Actually, I still think there is something here that would be useful for us and for our ministers. But maybe we need to think more about basic issues—like, what is the point of doing formal reviews? What are we trying to accomplish that can't be done just as well by our ministers and us just keeping an ear to the ground, so to speak?"

Sand Lake Church and its ministers were fortunate that its personnel committee had this important discussion. All too often, churches that have instituted staff reviews have done so without carefully exploring the reasons why a church might need formal reviews, and especially why those reasons might be substantially different from the reasons for having performance evaluations in secular workplaces. In addition, review processes all too often are put in place only when conflicts are brewing in the church, and the very act of conducting a review may unwittingly signal that "we have a serious problem, and our minister's job is on the line." In such cases, the review process itself can become a source of bitter conflict and a focal point for a power struggle, as it did in the example Marvin cited. In fact, that happens often enough that when I get a phone call or e-mail asking for a sample evaluation instrument or process, I ask first whether pressure is building among some church members who want to remove the minister. Are there people in this congregation who believe that conducting a review would help build a case against the minister that would force her or him to resign?

I have also known churches where a suspicion was abroad in the congregation that someone was trying to get rid of the minister, even though that was not the case. But the suspicion alone politicized the process. The result was division that did not need to happen. When such an incident occurs, an evaluation process may turn simmering tensions into brutal conflict.

When I am asked to consult with local churches about a review process, often I learn that someone among that church's lay leadership is drawing on a process he or she has used in a secular workplace—an instrument that has been slightly adapted for use by that congregation. Typically, these processes use a questionnaire that asks selected members for their evaluative opinions about various aspects of the work of the church's ministerial staff. Sometimes, the results are given only to a small circle of church officers. At other times, results are compiled and sent to every member of the congregation. No matter how the process is done or to whom results are reported, the evaluation process, more often than not, is awkward, embarrassing, and painful both for those being evaluated and for those who carry out the process.

Rather than being conducted as a regular, predictable part of the congregation's life, reviews of ministerial staff are often done sporadically. The consistency with which they are carried out tends to rise and fall with the enthusiasm for the task among members of the local church personnel committee or review committee. I am sure that somewhere in the whole of organized religion one can find congregations that embrace the idea of annual performance reviews with positive energy and have found that the process has brought about a marked improvement in their ability to carry forward God's mission. But they are rare. More often I encounter churches where performance reviews tend to be used because of vague notions that "we should do this," or "this will make our church more businesslike," or "all of us have to go through this where we work, so why shouldn't our ministers?" I have also seen less noble motives, such as a powerful person trying to use a review process to persuade one or more of the ministerial staff that it is time to retire or move elsewhere, or using a review to convince a majority of the congregation that the minister should leave.

In contrast to these congregations that evaluate their minister for all the wrong reasons, many local churches, out of an intuitive discomfort with the idea, do not conduct *any* kind of a review of ministerial staff. Smaller-membership churches (sometimes thought of as "family churches") tend to feel less pressure than larger churches to be businesslike—one factor in the avoidance of reviews as a regular practice. Considering the hazards of a poorly done review process, it may be wiser not to do one at all than to do it carelessly.

Hazards of Careless Reviews

Hazards? The discussion of the personnel committee at Sand Lake Church suggested many of the hazards. Let me name them explicitly:

1. Many performance evaluations in secular work settings tend to focus on *measurable outcomes*. For many secular jobs, measurable outcomes may be an important focus of a review, but this consideration does not translate easily into the work of a minister. Although a few measurable outcomes are related to the work of a minister (such as church income, growth in membership and attendance), these numbers are rarely the result of only the minister's work. (The next time someone wonders aloud who is responsible for people coming into the church, take a quick show-of-hands survey in your congregation. Ask, "How many of you trace the beginning of your life in the Church of Jesus Christ to a newspaper ad? How many to an attractive church building? How many to the influence

of a minister? How many to the influence of a member of the church, either from your family or from beyond your family?") It may be fair to ask, "What has been the role of our minister in our church finances, membership growth or loss, and attendance?" But it is extremely risky to draw conclusions about the work of the minister based on outcomes for which the minister is only partly responsible.

In addition, only a few people know many of the most important results of ministry. The teenager who was contemplating suicide but chose to live after a chance conversation with her minister may be the only one who knows about the impact of that conversation. The man who decided to go into a chemical-abuse recovery program after seeing his minister go through a recovery program may have never told even the minister. Certain life-and-death outcomes may not be apparent for years.

To include measurable outcomes in a review of a minister's work is not only unfair; in addition, it may place responsibility for these outcomes where it does not belong. A minister clearly has something to do with whether members are giving enough to carry forward the ministry and mission of the congregation, but that outcome rests primarily with the members of the church who decide from week to week and year to year how much to pledge and how much to give. A minister may have a great deal to do with whether people are motivated to become members or to show up on Sunday morning for worship, but the real decision makers are the members of the church who decide whether to show up and the potential members who decide whether to join.

Thus, a review process that relies on measurable outcomes runs the terrible risk that a minister may be held accountable for the spiritual sloth of the members of the congregation. Most ministers wish they could motivate people to fervent worship and generous giving, but the reality is that they have only limited power to change people's behavior.

2. Performance evaluations in secular work settings often measure performance against standards defined by the workplace. "Not necessarily so!" a friend recently said to me about his workplace. "Where I work, the standards of performance are anybody's guess." But a goal of good organizational management in secular

workplaces is exactly that—to define the standards as clearly as possible so that both supervisor and employee know whether the job is being done well.

To be sure, most denominations have a set of standards for candidates for ordination, as well as ethical standards by which continuing fitness for ministry may be judged. Helpful as they may be for their intended purposes, even these standards do little to help a local church measure the day-to-day competencies, behavior, or character of its ministerial staff.

It is the rare local church that has even made a stab at defining standards for the work required of its ministerial staff. Many have developed position descriptions, but usually those describe only *what* needs to be done, not how or at what level tasks should be done. But individual church members often do have their own ideas about standards, about how the various tasks of ministry should be done, and what priority should be given to these tasks.

Performance evaluations of local church ministers that include questions about how well certain tasks of ministry are being done may function as a Rorschach inkblot test does: they reveal far more about those who responded to the evaluation questions than they do about the clergy being evaluated. In worst-case scenarios, such performance evaluations can become divisive to the congregation and offer an opportunity for those with the loudest voices to impose their internal standards on an entire congregation, often to the detriment of the congregation and its ordained clergy.

3. Because performance reviews are generally not conducted with any regularity in a local church, the very process may create in the minds of some members a concern that there must be a problem with staff. "They must be getting ready to fire the minister," some will assume. "After all, isn't that what you do when you're trying to get rid of someone? You build a file, document what they have done wrong, and put it in the files so they can't come back and sue you for discrimination or something."

Long ago, scientific researchers learned that it is essential to design research methods that do not alter the data by the very process of observation. But they also learned how difficult, perhaps impossible, it is to avoid altering information by the act of observation. The same is true of carrying out performance reviews. The act of doing it can alter the information gathered about a staff member's performance.

Especially in congregations! *Especially* in congregations, where negative information tends to take on a life of its own, feed on itself, and become far more powerful than review leaders intended. Every middle-judicatory minister (conference or association minister, bishop, district superintendent, executive presbyter, and the like) has seen the bewildering phenomenon of a church going into "free fall"—a situation that begins with a few manageable disagreements with the pastor rapidly roaring out of control so that everything done by the pastor becomes a target of further criticism.

An ill-timed review process can trigger free fall, especially if the process includes an opportunity for anonymous responses from many people—responses that are then either formally reported to the whole congregation or fed back through the grapevine. The material, whether printed in an official report or passed along the grapevine, can feed a belief that "we are a broken and deeply divided church that has come to a standstill," when in fact any of the church's problems may have began as routine disagreements, solvable by people of good will.

4. Many performance evaluations run the risk of providing an opportunity for *scapegoating*. (Scapegoating is blaming one person for all the problems of a community. The psychospiritual logic is that if the person being blamed can be punished or run out of town, the community thinks that it will have solved all its problems. Even though scapegoating is an unhealthy strategy, it is often used by people who are unhappy with their own lives. Because it creates the illusion that community problems have been solved by throwing out the designated "troublemaker," it can become habitual behavior in some congregations.)

How might the performance evaluation of ministers provide an opportunity for scapegoating? One review form I have seen began by asking respondents to rate their own personal spiritual happiness, based on the question, "How happy are you with your spiritual life right now, on a scale of 1 to 5, with 1 being extremely happy and 5 being extremely unhappy?"

If you responded with a 1 or 2, which of the following contribute to your happiness? Please check all that apply:

___ our minister's sermons
___ the hymns our minister chooses
___ the pastoral prayer
___ pastoral care provided to you by our minister
___ other: _____

The next question was "If you responded with a 4 or 5, which of the following contribute to your unhappiness? Please check all that apply:" The same list followed.

That evaluation instrument provided an opening for some to claim, "I am spiritually unhappy, and my minister is to blame." Even healthy congregations have some members who take that attitude, and it won't matter to them what kind of review process the congregation uses. What may matter a great deal is whether such attitudes show up as data in a formal review process that informs decisions about the minister's work, and whether such attitudes can be responded to in a pastoral conversation.

Scapegoating happens in ministry often. In fact, anyone who is unduly offended at being blamed for what someone else did or didn't do probably shouldn't be in ministry. When people are tempted to blame their minister for their own unhappy feelings or experiences, I believe the healthiest response is to encourage these individuals to speak directly to their minister (or to whomever else they may blame) about their feelings. Such a conversation at least holds out a chance that the situation may be redeemed and that scapegoating may be averted. But if inappropriate blame is reported in a performance review, those conducting the review may draw wildly inaccurate conclusions about the minister's performance.

A church member once blamed a clergy colleague of mine for the affair this woman's husband was having. "You'll have to tell me more," said my colleague. "I don't quite see the connection between anything I have done or am doing and your husband's affair." The woman replied, "I come home from church so frustrated. My husband says he really *likes* your sermons, but if he likes them so much, why did he go off and have this affair? I keep thinking that if your sermons were more powerful and upheld what the Bible teaches about morality and family values, he would have had a stronger spiritual core and wouldn't have done this to me."

This began a life-changing dialogue. My colleague said to me, "Believe it or not, I did not mind a whole lot—well, maybe a little bit—being blamed in this instance, because it became the starting point for this family to deal with important issues. More important, this woman was willing to be honest directly with me about what she was feeling, and she hadn't gone all around the church saying what a lousy preacher I am."

Without that conversation, what might have happened if she had received a questionnaire asking respondents to evaluate the effectiveness of the pastor's preaching, as do some of the forms I have seen local churches use? What if she had responded anonymously, and her responses had been reported formally to a governing board or fed back through the grapevine when a member of the review committee forgot the group's policy of confidentiality?

Another colleague told me of being taken to task by a committee member who voiced extreme displeasure over the outcome of a children's ministries committee meeting the previous week. The issue before the committee was whether to hire an additional Sunday morning child-care worker for the church nursery, even though no money was budgeted for additional help. The minister was present at the meeting, but because she was comfortable with the way the discussion was going, she decided to stay out of the decision making. The next day, a committee member whose opinion did not prevail came in to see the minister and poured out her unhappiness. The minister replied, "Are you saying that I am responsible for the committee's decision not to hire a second child-care attendant for the nursery? Am I hearing that right?"

"Exactly!" said the committee member. "You had your chance to sway things in the right direction, but you blew it. Mary Jo said that we simply couldn't afford a second paid child-care attendant in the nursery, so it would be poor stewardship. Right then I really wanted you to say that a second child-care attendant would be great stewardship, a great investment, because it would be welcoming to all these new parents who have been showing up lately who want their children to be safe in our church nursery. But you just—well, you just *sat* there, and they decided not to hire a second attendant, which was *not* a good decision for the future of our church! You had a golden opportunity to use your influence for the good of the church, and you blew it!"

This outburst began a conversation extending off and on for several months, about how this member could claim her own voice. The minister pointed out that she herself could not and should not try to detect the unspoken thoughts and desires of committee members and speak those thoughts and desires on their behalf. This was an important conversation, one that no doubt was helpful to the member and to her committee. Again, I have wondered what would have happened if before (or instead of) that conversation, this committee member had received a questionnaire asking her to evaluate the minister's effectiveness in working with committees? An incident that became an opportunity for ministry might instead have easily been taken as evidence by a review committee that the minister had serious problems working effectively with church committees.

To be sure, a review may produce well-deserved negative responses requiring careful attention. But congregation members are like the rest of the human species: if we can find someone else to blame for our unhappiness, we will do so, at least publicly. Privately, many of us tear into ourselves with a loathing we rarely let others see. Our public blame of someone else as a cover for our own self-loathing plays itself out in congregational life in countless big and little ways, often with the minister becoming the temporary designated "blamee," or scapegoat. It is one of the costs of being a representative of the whole Body of Christ. Fortunately, we have ways through liturgy and counseling to work with this phenomenon. But when scapegoating shows up as data in a staff evaluation process, it becomes much harder to recognize and to work with redemptively.

5. Performance reviews run the risk of providing an avenue for *rage*, giving it far more power over the community than is acceptable. I credit church consultant Gail Dekker for her helpful distinction between anger and rage. *Anger* can be a positive force in community life. Anger is a sign that something is wrong—something is not as it should be. When anger is named and focused appropriately, it gives the community an opportunity to recognize what needs to be corrected and to work on the issue. By contrast, *rage* wants to hurt, to punish, and to punish some more. A person in the grip of rage is usually not interested in

solutions, only in retribution. Rage almost always arises from hurt, usually a perceived injustice. Rage has amazing endurance! Even if the hurt associated with rage is not always front and center, rage has a way of tucking itself into the corners of our memories and roaring out when a topic associated with that rage shows up.

Some people use rage as a mechanism for trying to build relationships. Strong bonds are often formed when people discover that they have a common enemy (the trick, of course, is to be sure there is always an "enemy" out there, because if there isn't, the bond quickly starts to erode). Tight bonds of sympathy also appear to be formed when raging people can convince others how badly they have been hurt by someone in power or authority, such as their pastor.

I don't have to go very far out on a limb to claim that even the world's kindest, gentlest congregation will have some folk who have been so badly hurt somewhere, sometime in their lives, that they have the capacity to act out of rage. Rage is so common that every minister needs to develop some strategies for hearing and responding to rage redemptively. But when rage shows up as data in a performance review of ministerial staff, it is extremely hard to interpret and can easily be given far more power than it should have over the life of the community.

6. Many performance reviews run the risk of bringing along with them less-than-helpful images and values from the popular culture about the nature of the church and its ministry, especially the image of consumerism. A clergy colleague once lamented to me, "People in our part of town select a church just as they select a lawn service! They sign on with those that promise the greenest grass for the cheapest price! How do we break through that habit and reclaim the sense that we are called as a community of faith to be in God's mission?"

That may be *the* question for religious leaders in our times. Because consumerist images permeate the church (at least in North America), I do not want to feed such images of the church and its ministry by carrying out a review process that asks, "On a scale of 1–10, how well are your spiritual needs being met by Reverend Doddering's sermons? His pastoral care? His 'Time for Children'? What are the five most important things you get from your membership in the church? Do you feel you are getting good value for the money you give?"

Sociologist Kirk Hadaway, in his recent book *Behold I Do a New Thing: Transforming Communities of Faith*, argues that church "is a place where people have personal transformation, wake up to the reality of God's Realm, and begin to grow in knowledge and understanding in a vocational, incarnational life. It is not a place where people are left unchanged and self-satisfied."[1] Client satisfaction surveys may be appropriate in settings where, by virtue of paying a fee, clients have in effect bought a package of services. But church members are not clients, and contributions of time and money are not fees for religious services. A review process that focuses primarily on how satisfied church members are with their minister is inconsistent with the historic purpose of the church and its ministry, and can almost be guaranteed to produce confusing and perhaps even polarizing results.

Often, although not always, those in charge of constructing and carrying out an evaluation of the minister are confident that they know what they are doing. Either they have administered a similar instrument in another setting, or they have been the subject of evaluation in their place of work. But no matter how well secular evaluation instruments may work in a secular setting, most do not translate well into measuring the functions of ministry. Trying to measure outcomes that are not easily measurable, evaluating against multiple, often competing internal standards, sending unintended negative messages about the health and well-being of the church and its relationship to its ministerial staff, scapegoating, empowering rage, and feeding consumerist images about the nature of the church and its ministry—these are real hazards. They come along like noxious aquatic weeds attached to the bottom of a boat when review processes are transported from settings where measurable outcomes are important, where performance standards are objectively defined, and where there is a legitimate expectation of getting good value for one's money. There are many review processes that work well in secular settings, but even when they offer wisdom for us to consider in the church, we need to be extremely cautious about translating processes and assumptions from secular settings into the church. Any review process or instrument should be assessed carefully with these hazards in mind to make sure the process avoids them as much as possible.

Another hazard of using certain evaluation instruments is the quality of information generated. If we think of the evaluation of ministers as a form of research in which information is sought to measure the effectiveness of work, two questions must be asked about the quality of the information gathered. One is the question of *reliability*: if we ask more than once for the same kind of information about the same staff person from the same congregation, will we get reasonably similar results? If the results vary wildly depending on who happens to be giving the information or even asking the questions, then the information is not reliable. Significant damage can be done to the relationship between minister and congregation if unreliable information is released to the whole congregation or becomes the basis for major decisions.

A second issue about the quality of the information is the question of *validity*—that is, does the information produced measure what it claims to measure, or does it represent something else? Many performance evaluations of ministers fail the test of validity. They tend to tell us far more about the values, beliefs, history, and psychological well-being of those who respond to evaluation questionnaires than they tell us about the work of the minister.

Why Should We Conduct a Review?

Good grief! With all these hazards in doing reviews of ministerial staff in a local church, is there *any* compelling reason to try to do anything like a review process?

Yes!

1. A good review process provides believable feedback about how the ministry of the whole church is going. Such feedback is essential to the healthy functioning of any local church and to the continued improvement of ministry.

No matter how carefully a minister may listen to the networks of information (choir rehearsal, fellowship groups, coffee hours), such informal listening is never quite enough to know about the full impact of the work of a single minister or about the ministry of a whole congregation. Good reviews *strategically* seek feedback for the purpose of empowering the ministry of the congregation.

2. A good review process is a reminder of where and to whom we are accountable. My own denomination recognizes three types of authorized ministry: ordained, commissioned, and licensed. Authorization for ministry always comes from an association—an organization of local churches and clergy within a designated geographical area and the first official expression of the church beyond the local congregation. Associations ordain, license, or commission ministers, and the official standing of authorized ministers is usually held in associations where those ministers live and serve. By a process known as "situational support conferences" (formerly known as periodic review), conducted by associations on behalf of the whole United Church of Christ, authorized ministers are held accountable for faithfulness to their vows of ordination, commissioning, or licensing. Even though specific steps of the situational support conferences vary widely from association to association, this review reminds authorized ministers of their accountability to the whole church through the association where they hold their standing.

Reviews of ordained ministers conducted by congregations focus on the accountability of clergy to that local congregation but must always be done with an awareness of the wider accountability expected of clergy. I once encountered an angry local church trustee who was upset with something his minister had done. "We hired him. We pay him. We are the only ones who have the right to tell him what to do," he said. "And we will fire him if he doesn't do what we tell him to do." I replied, "It is true that you called him, you pay him, and your congregation certainly can fire him. But keep in mind that you called someone who at the time of being ordained made some promises that are at the core of who he is. He is accountable to the whole church for keeping those promises. So just be sure that what you are asking him to do is in keeping with those promises he made when he was ordained."

The specific details of how ministers are accountable beyond the congregations that pay their salaries vary from denomination to denomination. Even in denominations that practice local-church ordination, an expectation prevails that ministers are accountable for their work more broadly than just to the congregation where they are employed.

Denominations like my own that have stressed individual freedom and autonomy of individual congregations sometimes attract ministers who aren't eager to be held accountable to anyone. I once heard these words from a seminary student who was already serving a small parish part time: "I *have* to have complete freedom of action in my ministry. I can't imagine having handcuffs put on me every time I turn around. It's *my* ministry!"

"Well," said a minister with 35 years of experience, on hearing the comment: "I think this congregation called you to minister *with* them and to help them carry out the ministry of the congregation. This church is not just the source of your salary and benefits so you can go off and do whatever you want to do."

A good review process also helps the congregation to be accountable to itself for what it has done and hasn't done. Being accountable is a vital spiritual discipline to keep us from frittering ourselves away to whatever feels good at the moment!

3. A good review process is a vital component in effective problem solving. Small issues that need attention can be identified soon enough that they can be addressed before they grow large and destructive. If issues are addressed in a timely manner, volunteer leadership of the local church and the ministerial staff have a much better chance of being partners in problem solving rather than adversaries in a power struggle.

4. A good review process is a vital component in the personal and professional health and growth of the ministerial staff. As I will describe later, the review process I recommend in local churches is little more than a strategy for gathering feedback for ministerial staff and for lay and/or volunteer leaders about the effectiveness of what they are doing. (The method could also be adapted for judicatories.) *Good feedback is to our community life what breathing and eating are to our biological lives. Without it, we simply do not function very well in community.*

Asking for good feedback is what this book is about! But first, in chapter 2, let's look at purpose and criteria. What is a good purpose for doing a review? How do we know that a review process we are considering will give us good feedback and avoid the hazards described in this chapter?

17

Note

1. C. Kirk Hadaway, *Behold, I Do a New Thing: Transforming Communities of Faith* (Cleveland: Pilgrim Press, 2000).

What Makes a Review a Good One?
Why Do It at All?

The chapters that follow include specific outlines for gathering feedback on ministerial leadership and the ministries of the church. I propose six criteria for designing a respectful, useful feedback process. Even if a local church decides to use some other method for carrying out reviews, these criteria may be used to assess any review process.

The Covenant

Reviews should be consistent with the nature of the covenantal relationship between pastor and congregation, and with a theological understanding of the nature of the church and its ministry. In my denomination, when we install someone as "pastor and teacher" of a congregation, the installation service speaks of the congregation's having been guided by the Holy Spirit to call this person to the office. Other denominations similarly refer to the sense that the Holy Spirit has somehow been involved in the call. This relationship began with a process of spiritual discernment, when a search committee and the congregation as a whole asked:

- What is God calling our church to be and do now and in the near future?
- What gifts for ministry do we need in our next ordained minister to help us carry out what God is calling us to be and do?
- Whom is God calling to be our next ordained minister?

This relationship is sustained by continued discernment of God's call to the congregation and to the minister. It is a relationship that affirms God's call to the entire congregation to ministry and mission (even if the congregation does not entirely understand this call). Ministry and mission are carried out not only by the paid staff. The role of the ordained minister is to guide, encourage, and teach the congregation in its ministry and mission. The congregation and minister covenant with one another and with God to be faithful together in fulfilling God's call.

The role of ordained ministers is carried out in varied ways, depending on the congregation and the minister. In some respects the ministerial role resembles other positions in our communities—executive director of a voluntary nonprofit agency, school principal, or director of a human-service organization. Because of these similarities between parish pastors and other leaders in our communities, we may come to think of the pastor's role in terms of these positions. But the church is not just another voluntary agency with a hired director, even though much of the congregation's work is done by unpaid volunteers. Nor is the church just another human-service organization with a professional executive, even though congregations address many human needs. Rather, *the church is a community of God called by God to witness to the transforming, life-giving love of God in a broken world. Authorized ministers are those called by God and the church to specific functions of leadership among the people of God.*

A review consistent with the covenantal relationship between clergy and congregation will avoid focusing only on how the minister is functioning as an employee. Rather, it focuses on how we are doing together in carrying out the various aspects of mission and ministry to which God calls all of us.

The Role of Communication

Reviews should be an example of healthy communication for the congregation. When we use the word "communication" in the church, we tend to think of "mass communication," especially through print and electronic media. I once offered for a cluster of churches a workshop titled, "Healthy Communications in the Congregation." At least two participants were disappointed because they had anticipated a workshop that would teach them how to improve their local church newsletter, how to set up a Web site, and how to use automatic dialing devices to inform members of upcoming church events. Obviously, I hadn't communicated well about the kind of communication I had in mind.

This criterion is not about newsletters, Web sites, telephone-dialing devices, or even about "telling our story so that more people understand who we really are." Although mass distribution of a message may be one part of "communication," I refer here to exchanges involving two or more people. I am thinking of the amazing event that occurs whenever a thought, image, or feeling forms in my brain (and in other parts of my body), and as a conscious being, I am aware of this thought, image, or feeling. I want you to experience in your mind and body a reasonable approximation of what is in mine. So with my voice or with my fingers, I speak or write some words or draw a picture representing the image, thought, or feeling, and I transmit that to you. Of course, what I transmit has a host of embedded meanings and signals. Then I perhaps pay careful attention to what you say or don't say, or what you do or don't do—in other words, to your feedback, to learn if what entered your brain and body seems reasonably close to what is in mine.

My thoughts, images, and feelings have to make their way through an astonishing array of psychic swamps and emotional briar patches in both of our minds before those thoughts or images safely reach you. It is essential that you give me feedback that in effect says, "Message safely arrived," or "Message badly damaged en route. Try again." But if you give me no feedback at all, I am left wondering: Did that thought, image, or feeling I tried to transmit actually arrive? And if it didn't, what *did* you think I said?

This need for feedback is the reason I think of complete communication as a circle. *Without good feedback, the circle of communication is incomplete.* Our communication with one another builds communities. It is the medium through which redeeming activity takes place. If the circle of communication is incomplete, the effectiveness of the church as a vehicle of God's love and mercy is compromised.

After you read the outlines for feedback/reflection groups in the chapters that follow, you may say, "This method is nothing fancier than simply giving good feedback to church leaders." You would be exactly right. What I propose is a strategy for completing circles of communication in situations when most churches fail to close the circle.

Here are some marks of healthy communications that should be embodied in a review process.

Speak for Yourself

In a culture of healthy communication, people are encouraged to tell their own stories and to let other people tell theirs. This is especially important in reporting dissatisfaction or unhappiness. It is unsettling when Charlie tells me, "Mary is greatly annoyed with you." Or: "Almost everyone was angry about that sermon you preached on Christmas Eve." Or: "Fred [chair of the deacons] thinks it is time for you to start looking for another call." Such comments are confusing because we don't know how accurate they may be. Also we don't know whether "almost everyone" really means "almost everyone" or represents only two or three people. Secondhand feedback may strain our relationships with the people named in these reports. The speaker is implying, "I have insider information that you don't have. *I* am the one who is really 'in the know,' not you." Receiving these reports secondhand, we may infer that the people named as critics do not trust us enough to speak with us directly about their issues. Such comments may reveal the speaker's own deep feelings or opinions, which he or she has projected onto others. It is important that Mary, "almost everyone," and Fred be encouraged to tell their own stories, rather than letting someone else deliver the message.

I remember being called to meet with a congregation whose relationship with its minister was under severe strain. More than half of the active members showed up for the meeting. I didn't know what to expect, but feared I would hear a lot of blaming and attempts to report what other people were feeling. "Tell me what you have experienced," I said. To my amazement and great relief, with only one exception, for the next hour I heard only firsthand stories. No one tried to speak for anyone else. No one tried to tell anyone else's story or report on what "everyone" was thinking or feeling. I came away from that meeting convinced that despite the trauma this congregation had experienced, not only would it survive—it would thrive because the congregants appeared to have learned this habit of healthy communication. A good review process encourages people to tell their own stories and avoids seeking secondhand or thirdhand reports.

DON'T ACCENTUATE THE NEGATIVE

In a culture of healthy communication, people are encouraged to avoid "awfulizing." That is, people do their best to speak the truth without exaggerating negative experiences to suit their own needs. People "awfulize" in relating their experience with someone perceived as more powerful, expanding the incident in the telling to imply that the person in power has harmed them out of either malice or stupidity. For the "awfulizer," the payoff is either to receive sympathy from others ("You poor dear, he treated you so badly") or to be seen as a hero for outwitting the knucklehead in power.

A bishop once had to intervene in a local church where a retired minister, a member of the congregation, had started an unofficial, somewhat clandestine Monday-morning discussion group. The meeting had become a time to shred the sermon the current pastor had preached the day before. Although the clergy code of ethics in that denomination gave the bishop grounds for bringing formal disciplinary charges against the retired minister for interfering in the work of the new leader, the bishop decided that an informal conversation would be more effective.

"John," said the bishop, "your Monday-morning group is having a negative effect on the work of the congregation and the current minister. In the past month, four church members have called me, complaining about comments the current minister made from the pulpit. Each of these callers either quoted you directly or spoke about statements they attributed to you. Seems as though most of what people are reporting comes out of your Monday-morning group. I think it's healthy to have lively discussion about the sermons, but these calls have made me wonder how appropriate you have been with your criticisms of your current minister."

"But Bishop," John shot back, "I'm just a member of the church and want to claim my right to be an involved church member. All I want is to be an active, concerned member."

The bishop said, "Well, it's too bad, I think, if this is what you believe being an effective church member means. But like it or not, you are always ordained, even in retirement, and as such, that gives you a degree of power and authority in that church, or in any church, that others don't have. It sounds to me as though you are tearing into every sermon pretty hard, and that is something I would hope no member of the church would do. I would especially hope that an ordained person wouldn't do that. You have to be sensitive to the measure of power and authority you have, for good or for harm, by virtue of your ordination."

Two months later, the bishop learned that John had discontinued the Monday-morning group and had also stopped coming to church. John had written a letter to the Monday-morning group and to a selected number of others in the congregation, saying that he had been "silenced" and thrown out of the church by the bishop, who "left me with a veiled threat to take away my ordination, and therefore my pension."

John was practicing extreme "awfulizing." ("See what that mean-spirited bishop did to me! I won't ask you outright to feel sorry for me, but that's really what I'm encouraging by making it seem that I have become the innocent victim of a powerful bishop. Having you feel sorry for me makes me feel good. This is how I make friends.") Awfulizing doesn't always involve such distortions of truth, but may consist "only" of an overdramatic account of how badly the speaker has been treated by a person in power.

It is not always easy to distinguish between awfulizing and legitimate complaints about the allegedly powerful, but one way to tell the difference is to watch what the speaker does with the complaint. Does he tell his sad story to other people in the absence of the person in power, thereby winning a payoff, either sympathy or a hero's medal? Does she talk about her complaint in a way that portrays the person in power as evil or as a fool? Or does she take the complaint directly to the powerful person and tell it in a way that allows a good-faith effort to resolve the issue?

Awfulizing is common in our society and is particularly flagrant in our political process ("These special-interest groups are ruining our lives! I am the only candidate who will stand up to them and reclaim your rightful voice.") But let's not bring it into the church. When we do so, we reduce the positive benefits of good communication among members. Awfulizing in the church damages the ability of a congregation and its ministers to carry forward the church's ministry and mission.

A good review process is one that encourages concerns to be voiced in a way that allows a good-faith effort to resolve problems.

SPEAK UP!

In a culture of healthy communication, people are encouraged to say what they need to say to those who need to hear it. Many years ago a woman named Sandy, member of a local church my wife and I were serving as co-pastors, gave me one of the nicest gifts I had received in ministry up to that time. We were new in that church and had not yet caught on to which aspects of church life were more or less claimed by certain members as their areas of ministry. Out of ignorance, I goofed. I knew the church council wanted to sponsor an all-church sit-down Harvest Dinner. I knew that Mary Ellen, another member, had expressed some interest in organizing such an event, so I asked her if she would be willing to take charge of the dinner. She quickly agreed. What I didn't know was that for years Sandy was the informal but steady coordinator for special church dinners. It was her love, she was good at it, and an unwritten understanding prevailed that this was Sandy's ministry (and her domain!).

A couple of weeks after I asked Mary Ellen to coordinate the dinner, Sandy came to see me. She was obviously distressed. "Pastor," she began, "this is really hard for me to do, but I have to find out. Why did you ask someone else to coordinate the Harvest Dinner? I thought that planning big dinners was something the church wanted *me* to do. I would have been happy to work with Mary Ellen, but now I just wonder if I haven't been doing it very well all along and I'm just not supposed to be involved?" All of a sudden some lights clicked on in my head.

"Oh, Sandy, I am so sorry," I said. "I didn't realize this was something you had been asked to do, and somehow it just never came up when I was talking with others. No one is unhappy with your work in the past! I certainly wasn't trying to send you a message about anything."

"Well, OK," she said with a sigh. "That helps. Tell you what— I'll call Mary Ellen and see if she could use a hand with anything. And, oh, by the way, I want you to know I haven't said a word about this to anyone in the church. I figured this was something between you and me—at least that's how it seemed to me—so I decided you were the one I needed to talk to about this."

"Sandy, thank you so much," I said. "I really, really appreciate your trusting me enough to let me know how you were feeling. I think we'll get along just fine."

Our trust in each other and respect for each grew enormously in that brief interchange. I knew I could count on her to be open and honest with me, and that she would never build an alliance against me by complaining about me to someone else. Equally important, I think Sandy learned that she could be honest with me and that I would not retaliate if she shared a negative concern with me.

Doing what Sandy did is hard for many people. I think it is hard because people fear the loss of a relationship if they state their negative feelings or disagreements face-to-face. Sometimes, sadly, those fears are well founded. In the best of all worlds, I would be delighted if we all could trust each other enough to be able to speak honestly and openly, and if we never damaged relationships by doing so. We are not there yet.

But we can develop enough self-discipline to recognize the great harm done to relationships when John complains to Mary about Susan, with the result that John and Mary develop an alliance against Susan. Then Mary gets caught thinking that she has to fix the issue between John and Susan, and Susan may be the last to know that John has a complaint about her. What a tangle!

Pastoral relations committees or pastor-parish relations committees have bought unnecessary trouble by presenting themselves to their congregations as the "complaint department." "You've got a complaint about the pastor? Tell a member of our committee. You don't have to use your name. Just let us know, and we'll straighten things out." I exaggerate only slightly. No wonder such committees tend to be frustrated and baffled about their role. Unwittingly, in their efforts to build positive relations between congregation and minister, committee members have invited the congregation to employ unhealthy triangulation. Then they wonder what went wrong when their system doesn't work.

A good review process is one that encourages people to say what needs to be said to those who need to hear it. Those who conduct a review should take care not to portray it as the only occasion when church members provide helpful feedback. Rather, the reviewing group should present the review as an example of the healthy communication that can take place all the time in this congregation.

LISTEN UP!

In a culture of healthy communication, people believe that listening carefully is as important, sometimes more important, than speaking articulately. When people listen carefully, they close the circle of communication by paying attention to feedback. Everyone involved in communication must listen carefully. This attention honors the other person by ensuring that her or his thoughts are accurately received. "What we need in our church," said a church member whose congregation had struggled with one conflict after another, "is less debate and more dialogue. More listening and less speech-making."

Why does it seem so difficult to listen well to one another? Sometimes we don't listen well because we are paying more attention to our own responses, or to the defense we will offer, than we are to the other person's words. Sometimes we may not like the speaker, and we believe that listening carefully will make us feel that we are giving in or giving up. Sometimes we don't listen well because we are distracted, tired, or impatient. Sometimes we are afraid of losing the friendship of others who may oppose the speaker. All these reasons and more contribute to poor listening, which in turn leads to blaming, shaming, ridiculing, and belittling. These responses rarely contribute positively to a church's ability to communicate about hard issues. They have no place in a good review process.

Helpful reviews in the church require careful, respectful listening. They can and should become an example to the church about how the congregation benefits when good listening is woven into the church's habits of communication. In congregations where careful, respectful listening is the norm, people whose views are far apart can engage hard topics without destroying the community. Problems facing the congregation can be dealt with much more effectively when congregants communicate well. In congregations that have learned how to listen well, members experience a depth in their relationships with one another that likely would not have been possible if the circle of communication were chronically incomplete.

In a culture of healthy communication, when something prompts anger, people will use their anger as an opportunity for seeking a solution rather than for hurting or destroying the other.

In a culture of healthy communication, people avoid blaming or shaming others. Little that is useful or good can be accomplished through either of these practices.

Timeliness as Indispensable

Reviews should provide timely information. If I am inadvertently causing harm or uncalled-for discomfort to another, and I don't learn the effects of my words or actions for a year or more, I have both caused unneeded discomfort and continued to practice the errant behavior in the meantime. The longer I practice such behavior, the harder it is to change when I finally learn that a change is necessary. The sooner I learn what is going well and what isn't, the sooner I can adjust what needs to be adjusted and the more confidence I can have in what I am doing well.

In the field of program evaluation, one method is called *responsive evaluation*. Evaluators conduct strategic, limited evaluations of specific components of a program while it is under way rather than waiting for one large evaluation at the end of the program. The idea is that what is learned can be fed back into the program as it continues. This is more or less the approach I outline in chapter 3 to meet the criterion of timeliness.

The Value of Reliable Information

Reviews should provide reliable and valid information. I mentioned earlier how hard it is to figure out what certain responses really mean in a review questionnaire. "Reverend Goforth preaches really good sermons. (I can hear and understand every word she says.)" "Reverend Goforth is an effective preacher. (She never goes beyond 12 minutes.)" "Reverend Goforth is a poor preacher. (Her sermons are so short that they suggest she doesn't much care about preaching.)" "Reverend Goforth is a great preacher! (Her personal stories are memorable, and I can see myself in them.)" "Reverend Goforth is a weak preacher. (She relies too much on personal stories and not on challenging theological concepts.)"

To obtain high-quality information, I urge that review processes ask for *descriptive information* as much as possible rather than *evaluative information.* The distinction is crucial. By "descriptive information" I mean simply that people are invited to describe their firsthand experiences as they have taken part in various aspects of the church's mission and ministries. They are *not* asked to evaluate (that is, place a value on their minister's behavior), *not* asked to rate, *not* asked to critique, *not* asked to assess. They *are* asked, with the help of some questions to open the discussion, to describe what they themselves, not someone else, experienced. From time to time, as people describe their own experiences, they may report that when they participated in a particular ministry of the church, they spent most of their time wishing they were somewhere else. Unless those people are lying, that is useful information. Such a response is different from "It was a bad program."

EVALUATIVE OR DESCRIPTIVE?

If you are considering a review instrument that uses a scale or asks people to rate or rank items, be aware that this form is asking for evaluative information. The information generated by such a survey is likely to be ambiguous. Why? To evaluate, we have to make comparisons. How does this experience we are asked to evaluate compare to some standard? But the problem is that members asked to evaluate their minister are likely to have many different standards. Two participants may give the same answer on one item, but their answers don't necessarily mean the same thing. It is also possible to get opposite answers to an evaluative question from people using the same standard. Remember the discussion of the Sand Lake UCC personnel committee in chapter 1? Dale said he thought his ministers were good preachers because they made him think and presented challenging ideas. But he knew someone else in the congregation who thought they were poor preachers for exactly the same reason.

To be sure, some aspects of church life may be evaluated against commonly held, more-or-less objective standards. We have standards for handling money, for ensuring building safety, for preventing abuse, for maintaining the buildings, and the like. Most insurance companies that insure churches provide good resources for conducting an audit of matters related to safety and liability. In addition, all, or virtually all, denominations expect certain ethical standards of their clergy, and it is possible to measure some kinds of ministerial behavior against those standards. But beyond these areas of institutional management and ethical behavior, members of congregations tend to have substantially different standards for what constitutes good ministry. This tendency makes it difficult to interpret the results of a performance evaluation that asks members to rate the effectiveness of their ministers.

Evaluative information may also be used inappropriately by those with the strongest opinions and the loudest voices, those who control the congregation and its minister, or would like to. Evaluative instruments may be used to make claims about support for or lack of support for the minister, or support for or lack of support for certain programs.

Descriptive information about our own firsthand experiences comes about as close as we are going to get to reliable and valid information. To be sure, when we ask for descriptive information, we will always get people's interpretations of their experiences, but that is all right. All experience is interpreted experience.

But wait, some may argue. If we give out 50 questionnaires asking people to rank the effectiveness of our minister's sermons, and 45 come back saying that the sermons are ineffective, doesn't that tell us something?

Of course it does. It tells us that 45 people think the sermons are ineffective. But this information alone is not likely to help the minister know what needs to be done differently, if anything. Indeed, the most predictable outcome will not be more effective sermons but rather an increase in the minister's anxiety or defensiveness about preaching.

But wait. Again, others will wonder: Aren't we prone to misreading or misunderstanding even our own experiences? Of course. Out of sheer politeness, Shelly may report, "I hung on every word of your sermon, Reverend Jones," when in fact she tuned out after the first minute and started wondering what it would be like to file for bankruptcy. Or, again, complete honesty about our experiences may be too embarrassing to share with others. Fred, for example, when asked to talk about what he experienced during the offering, may state that he was quietly mindful of his many blessings, although he was actually thinking lustful thoughts about an alto in the choir. Or, again, fear of appearing foolish may skew what we say about our experiences. Mary, for example, may report that she followed along in her own Bible during the scripture readings and always enjoys doing so, when, in fact, she spent most of the time looking for Deuteronomy in the New Testament.

Despite our tendency to use creative imagination as we report our own experiences, asking people to report their personal experience of church life still comes out far ahead in the quest for reliable information. We're looking for descriptions more than evaluations, in large part to raise the quality of the information upon which we base certain decisions, and to minimize the undue power and suasion in the church that may be held by a few with strong opinions.

Affirmation Motivates

Reviews should be respectful. Reviews should provide plenty of opportunity for affirmations about what is going well. Affirmations genuinely offered tend to generate confidence, and confidence tends to generate more effective ministry. Actually, that is true in all areas of our lives. Our desire to do something better is almost always more strongly motivated by being told we have already done something well, rather than by being told how poorly we have done it.

It is a terrible thing to see a review process generate vicious attacks on a minister. A review may uncover reasons why a minister should either consider another ministry setting or should consider a profession other than that of ordained ministry. But except in cases of egregious misconduct by ministers (and even then, they deserve respectful treatment), pastors do not need to be driven out at the cost of their own sense of call to ministry or their self-esteem.

KEEP NEGATIVE INFORMATION CONTAINED

Reviews should be proportional. When a review uncovers negative information, considerable care should be taken to ensure
that the negative information is contained and does not feed on
itself and take on greater life and power than it deserves. When a
negative comment appears in a review, it is tempting for those
responsible for conducting the review to start digging on their
own to see if they can confirm what appeared in the review.
Such an approach can inadvertently contribute to a sense of panic
that something terrible must be going on between the minister
and some in the congregation. When panic and anxiety take hold
of a congregation, people tend to view everything the minister
does with suspicion.

Negative information can and should be followed up on, but
great care must be taken so that follow-up encourages healthy
habits of communication in the congregation. Suggestions for
such follow-up are included in chapter 3.

A Framework for Enhancing the Value of Reviews

Reviews of the work of the ministerial staff are always more useful to the ministers and to the congregation when these elements
are also in place:

- mission, vision, and identity statements for this congregation;
- a carefully worded constitution and by-laws for the
  congregation that contain in broad outline this
  congregation's understanding of the duties and roles
  of officers, boards, and committees, and of its ministerial staff;
- position descriptions for all paid staff positions;
- a regular planning cycle in which the congregation as
  a whole, groups within the congregation, and staff all
  establish goals, objectives, and priorities related to the
  fulfillment of the mission of the congregation;
- regular reports to the governing body on progress in
  meeting those goals, objectives, and priorities;

- regular attention by the governing body to whether officers, boards, committees, and ministerial staff have the resources necessary to do what is asked of them.

It is beyond the scope of this book to elaborate in detail on these items. For now it is enough to say that any time a congregation wants to review its ministerial staff, it should also review the items listed above. When these elements are not in place or are not widely embraced by the congregation, the minister becomes unnecessarily vulnerable to the views of those in power. Indeed, in the absence of these elements, power is likely to be vested in assertive people, regardless of whether they hold an office, rather than being vested in the office.

Vision, mission, and identity statements should be reviewed regularly. They tend to have about a three-year life, sometimes less if they are buried in a closet, sometimes more if they are printed on the front of the weekly worship bulletin. Even if the statements themselves need no change after about three years, the sense of ownership decreases as new people come in and as long-term members die or move away.

Constitutions and by-laws and position descriptions also seem to have about a three-year life, no matter how good they are when adopted. Changing realities in the congregation and its community may call for adjustments in how the congregation and its minister carry out their mission. My wife and I once served as co-pastors of a congregation that had written into its constitution and by-laws a requirement that those documents be reviewed at least every five years. This wise provision helped to keep those governing documents alive and current.

A good *planning cycle* generates the ideas and perspectives for keeping a church's governing documents fresh. Some planning processes breathe vitality into a church, and some are a waste of time because the results gather dust and too often resemble a flight of fantasy rather than a realistic, thoughtful plan with *this* congregation and its setting in mind. I advocate plans designed for no more than two or three years: good plans include the ongoing day-to-day work that everyone knows will take place in this congregation. The plans include goals (i.e., compass points that may be restated from one planning cycle to another), objectives (specific, targeted outcomes), and priorities (what will deliberately be given more time than other things in this planning cycle) for the congregation, groups within the congregation, and the ministerial staff. A good plan also identifies the resources available to accomplish the plan, and it assigns responsibility for implementation. Ideally, the goals, objectives, and priorities are affirmed by the whole congregation, and become the outline for reporting by leaders to the congregation throughout the year. These reports include information not only about what is being done to implement the plan but also about whether resources are adequate to accomplish the plan.

This process most often breaks down when churches get excited about long-range planning, invest a great deal of time and energy into developing a long-range plan—and do it once. Then enthusiasm for the effort fades, memories of the plan grow dim, no one knows whether a planning process will ever be undertaken again, and people keep on doing what they have always done. Old habits live long.

What is the purpose of a review of ministerial leadership in the church? If a congregation observes carefully the criteria for reviews outlined in this chapter, but still is baffled about the purpose of doing a review, it will be difficult for the group in charge of evaluation to construct and conduct a satisfactory review process.

In the secular world, performance reviews are often linked to decisions about salary increases, advancement, and continued employment. The possibility of a salary increase and advancement is considered the primary incentive for excellence in work. Performance reviews document the performance and presumably help to determine whether and how much an employee should be rewarded with added salary, a promotion, or job security.

For the church, I urge that reviews *not* be tied to salary increases. I know few ministers who are motivated to improve the quality of their work by the possibility of a salary increase. For most ministers whom I know and work with, the desire to grow in competence and effectiveness almost always grows out of a yearning to be faithful to their call to ministry. Most clergy anticipate that salary increases will come in due time. They expect that salaries will be fair and will reflect the congregation's ability to pay. But few expect that increases will come as a reward for increased effectiveness in ministry, as documented by a review process. A review conducted to determine whether to grant salary increases and how large any raises should be, misses the point of the church and its ministry.

I believe that the purpose of reviews done in congregations is *to provide to ministerial staff and lay leaders reliable and valid feedback about how their work is going, so that they may strengthen the congregation's ministry and mission.* This purpose statement is so simple that I am almost embarrassed by its simplicity! It assumes that ministers and lay leaders will welcome reliable and valid feedback and will take it into account as they carry out their work. But simple as it may be, high-quality feedback is essential to the health of congregations. When congregations and their ministers cross swords, one of the most significant missing ingredients is high-quality feedback.

I don't believe for an instant that a review process that provides reliable and valid feedback for ministers and lay leaders, and that observes all the criteria I have suggested in this chapter will bring in heaven on earth. But I do believe that a healthy process will contribute greatly to the well-being of the congregation. A review should never be done carelessly or as an occasional afterthought.

How Does "Completing the Circle" Work?

"Completing the Circle" is made up of five broad stages. Small groups are at the heart of this process. The small groups come together to offer descriptive feedback about what group members have experienced in certain areas of congregational life. I call these groups "feedback/reflection" groups, ("feedback" because that is what participants are providing, and "reflection" because they examine their own experiences); but one church calls the groups "listening circles," and another calls them "circle sessions." The five broad stages are:

1. Planning the process
2. Gathering quality feedback
3. Discerning what the feedback means
4. Reporting findings
5. Assimilating the results into congregational life

1. Planning the Process

To launch "Completing the Circle," the person or group in charge of implementing it needs to do sufficient planning. It is worth investing time and energy into planning the process, because without well-laid plans, "business as usual" will claim so much time and attention that this or any other review process will be chronically postponed.

Unless a congregation's by-laws specify who will conduct reviews, the governing board should either assign responsibility for the process to an existing group or create a group specifically for this purpose. In churches that have both a personnel committee that oversees employment issues and a pastoral relations committee (or pastor-parish relations committee) that tends to the relationship between minister and congregation, it may not be obvious who should organize and carry out this process. Should it be the personnel committee, since the process will include reviews of the work of the clergy staff? Or should it be the pastoral relations committee because this process will reveal much about the relationship of the minister and the congregation, and, one hopes, will strengthen that relationship? I can easily argue either side of this question.

If a congregation's personnel committee has been asked to conduct regular reviews of the minister, then let that group use "Completing the Circle" as its review process. But the pastoral relations committee might also find this process helpful. In fact, I first developed the seeds of this process for pastoral relations committees whose members were frustrated that their congregations regarded them as the "complaints committee." "Completing the Circle" provides a clear strategy for changing a committee's focus and methodology. On the other hand, in some congregations, the pastoral relations committee is primarily a support group for the minister, and the committee does not ask for or accept complaints about the clergy. If that is the case, this committee may have a full agenda already, and it may be wise to assign responsibility for "Completing the Circle" to some other group.

I know of several congregations that formed a special review committee made up of former officers or former members of boards or committees. The logic here is that these people have enough recent knowledge of the mission and ministries of the congregation that they can act knowledgeably, but they don't have several other church-related responsibilities competing for their time and attention.

Once it is clear who is responsible for the reviews, this oversight group should familiarize itself with the entire "Completing the Circle" process by reading this book and discussing it enough that all group members understand the concepts and procedures. The oversight group can itself have the experience of being a feedback/reflection group by inviting a competent outsider who knows the process to lead a session. Or an oversight group member may be willing to moderate one session, using one of the discussion guides for feedback/reflection groups (see chapter 4). Either option would be help-ful. By having its own experience of being a feedback/reflection group, the oversight group will increase its ability to teach the con-gregation about the process, and strengthen its ability to develop a comprehensive "Completing the Circle" plan. Assuming that over-sight group members will moderate feedback/reflection sessions, they will be more effective in that role after having their own expe-rience as a session participant.

BEGINNING THE WORK

The oversight group will need to identify people willing to moderate feedback/reflection groups. I recommend that mem-bers of the oversight group be the primary source of leader-ship, but other congregation members may be invited if they have the gift of leading a small-group discussion in ways that inspire confidence. Leaders from outside the oversight group should be strongly urged to read this book to understand the process and the concepts.

Once the oversight group has immersed itself in this process sufficiently to be comfortable explaining it to others, it should ask for time on the agenda of the governing body. The oversight group should explain that church members will be invited from time to time to attend a feedback/reflection group. A moderator will lead people in discussing what they experienced in a desig-nated aspect of congregational life.

Information from feedback/reflection groups will be orga-nized into reports that go to the governing body, to staff people, and to leaders of program areas as needed, with the hope that the reported feedback will be taken into account as plans for church programs and ministry are developed. Any negative feedback will be shared with those in the best position to rem-edy the problem or incident that prompted the negative com-ments.

IDENTIFY PROGRAMS RIPE FOR REVIEW

The broader the ownership of the "Completing the Circle" process and concepts, the better. If it would be consistent with decision-making procedures in your congregation, ask the governing body to approve or affirm the use of this process. I think it is a good idea to ask for that approval and recommend you do so.

The next step is to identify the aspects of congregational life about which reliable feedback is most needed, and to determine how many feedback/reflection groups to schedule in one year. These two decisions may need to be made at the same time, and only after consulting with the governing body. I recommend that the oversight group and the ministerial staff develop a review plan for *at least* a year at a time.

Here are some central questions to consider:

- From which programs and ministries do we most want and need feedback during the next year or so?
- Does the chatter on our informal grapevine suggest that a certain program needs special attention?
- Do we suspect that a particular area of ministry should be greatly expanded?
- What program or ministry have we been conducting for a long time that now appears to be receiving less and less support?
- Is there some ministry or other activity that the ministers do regularly, while wondering whether they are doing it well, or whether they should be doing it at all?
- How do the people of our congregation respond to the various roles and tasks we expect of our ministers?
- How do the people of our congregation respond to the competence with which our minister handles ministerial tasks?
- Is there any yearning in the hearts of our members that we have not been responding to?

Most churches could conduct a feedback/reflection group on a different topic every day of the year and not run out of good material—clearly an impractical idea. I am mindful of the risks of wearing people out, especially the conveners. I generally recommend no more than a dozen groups a year for most churches (*not* a dozen for each program area). Congregations will find a frequency that works for their size and energy.

DEVELOPING A SCHEDULE

Congregations that use "Completing the Circle" will find their own equilibrium about how often they need to hold feedback/reflection groups for the process to generate the greatest benefit. Even if a church does nothing else with this process, holding three or four feedback/reflection groups in a year on individuals' experience of worship will produce a great deal of enlightening information. Since worship is the congregation's most important and most frequent activity, feedback about how people experience worship will also reveal much about the pulse of the congregation. (You say you don't know how often you could endure hearing Fred ask why we don't sing "Onward, Christian Soldiers" and "The Battle Hymn of the Republic"? Just be sure Fred is invited only once!)

I think it makes good sense for a congregation to develop a three-year "Completing the Circle" plan. Although not required, a plan gives the oversight group, ministerial staff, and other lay leaders a better chance to think comprehensively about congregational life. Are we asking for feedback from the areas of congregational life that have the greatest impact on who we are and what we do? Over time, are we going to get as full a picture as possible about what people experience in and because of our congregation?

Here is a sample three-year "Completing the Circle" plan indicating how much attention each area of church life will receive:

Year One
- Worship, four times during the year.
- Christian education for children and youth, including confirmation, once in midseason, and once at the end of the spring term.
- All elected boards and committees of the church, once for each board or committee during the year, about five to six months after newly elected people take office.

Depending on the number of elected boards and committees, this plan might provide for a total of 10 to 12 feedback/reflection groups in the year.

Year Two
- Worship, four times during the year.
- Recipients of pastoral care, once during the year. (The oversight group should be sensitive to issues of confidentiality. As the discussion guide in the next chapter makes clear, participants should be told right away that the no one will pressure them to respond if issues come up that they would rather not discuss with the group.)
- Outreach projects, one time per project during the year. (This feedback/reflection group would include members of the congregation who participated in the identified outreach project. If feasible, include people who have been involved in a project but who are not members of the congregation.)
- Evangelism and new members, once during the year. (This group would include new members who have joined during the past two years. It would be useful to include people who joined and became active, as well as those who joined and soon became inactive.)

Depending on the number of outreach projects, this listing might result in a total of eight to 10 sessions for the congregation in the second year.

Year Three
- Worship, four times during the year.
- Fellowship groups (women's, youth, for example), one time per group during the year.
- Special events and seasonal programs (Lent, Advent), once after each event or season. (How sessions are organized depends on the kind of programming done by a congregation during special seasons. For example, if a congregation offers midweek dinners followed by a speaker each week during Lent, holding a feedback/reflection group within a month after Easter would be a good idea. A group made up of some of those who attended one or more of these dinners will provide fresh feedback for those who will plan similar events next year.)

Depending on the number of events and fellowship groups, there might be from six to twelve groups for the entire congregation in this third year.

But wait! Why doesn't this three-year plan include a specific review of the church staff—the ordained ministers and other staff? Does this process only review programs? Although a church using "Completing the Circle" could establish feedback/reflection groups to gather feedback about how people have experienced their minister, the sample plan I outlined above asks for feedback from the areas of congregational life where most ministers devote most of their time. These include planning and leading worship, teaching, working with church boards and committees, providing pastoral care, guiding and leading outreach work, inviting new people to consider membership in this congregation, and relating to fellowship groups. The work of the ministers and other staff is reviewed—in a way that allows for reflection within the full context of the activity being explored.

2. Gathering High-Quality Feedback

In "Completing the Circle," feedback/reflection groups are the source of reliable and valid feedback and the centerpiece of the process. These groups consist of about eight to twelve people, usually members of the congregation, who are invited to meet for an hour to an hour and a half, describing what they have experienced in the aspect of congregational life that is the group's focus. Feedback/reflection groups are convened by a leader who guides the discussion. Ideally, a recorder takes notes on the discussion. Groups use a discussion guide (see samples in chapter 4) to help them start the conversation and to keep it on track. The oversight group I described earlier in this chapter provides the leader, the recorder, and the discussion guide. Because feedback/reflection groups are not intended to build alliances against the minister or to keep secrets from him or her, it is almost always advisable that a minister be present. In multiple-staff churches, usually the minister who has had primary responsibility for the program area under discussion should attend.

For some feedback/reflection groups, a specific target population should be invited. For example, when discussion focuses
on the confirmation program, current and recent members of
the confirmation class and their parents are the obvious people
to invite. Or again, when a board or committee decides to review its own work, committee members and perhaps some
who are affected by the committee's work become a feedback/
reflection group.

For other feedback/reflection groups, the target population is the entire congregation—for example, the groups that
focus on the experience of worship. For these groups, it usually works better to invite specific people to be part of a feed-
back/reflection group rather than to issue a general "y'all
come" invitation—and for several reasons. First, attendance
tends to be more predictable if the invitation is specific. The
sample letters of invitation and suggestions for inviting people
in chapter 4 include asking people to indicate whether they
will attend. The oversight group can invite more people if only
two or three people say they plan to attend. Second, over time,
specific invitations will tend to increase the chances that a
representative sample of the whole congregation will be heard.
Third, a "y'all come" invitation will tend to bring either those
who come (as they do to most activities) from a sense of duty
or those who have a complaint to air. Groups made up of only
these two kinds of folk may provide skewed feedback that does
not accurately reflect the congregation.

How might feedback/reflection groups be put together
when the target population is the whole congregation? In the
case of worship feedback/reflection groups, it might be wise to
begin by asking the body in the church that has oversight for the
worship life of the church (deacons, spiritual life committee, or
whomever) to be a feedback/reflection group once a year. In addition, groups of about eight to twelve people may be assembled
in a variety of ways.

If the oversight team desires that over time these feedback/
reflection groups will be a representative sample of the congregation as a whole, then a process of random selection may be
used. The theory of random selection is that every member of

the target population has an equal chance of being selected. No single feedback/reflection group will itself be a representative sample of the congregation, but over time, the more groups that come together, the greater the chances that the congregation will be fairly represented.

One church that uses this process prepared a sign-up chart with meeting times for the feedback/reflection groups on worship. This church's oversight group determined that four groups a year on worship experiences would be about right. The group members chose four dates that would fit what they knew of the congregation's calendar. They decided to hold three of the four immediately after worship, and one on a Tuesday evening. The sign-up chart had 12 slots under each meeting date. Members of the oversight group had decided early on that they would not do one-on-one recruiting for any session for which at least eight people had signed up. They also decided that 12 was an absolute upper limit. People were invited to sign up for a time that would work best for them. Members were told over and over that "we would really like for everyone in the church to participate in at least one of these sometime over the next two years." People were also asked to sign up for only one session to begin with. They were told that they could sign up for another if slots were still available a week before the scheduled session. This chart was circulated through the congregation during worship, board meetings, potlucks, and the like, until it filled up.

PUTTING CONGREGANTS IN THE PICTURE

No matter how feedback/reflection groups are put together, and whether the target population is the entire congregation or a specific group, the oversight team should keep several points in mind as it teaches the congregation about this process.

First, describe the overall process to the entire congregation over and over, through newsletters, spoken announcements, and other forms of communication. Many people will need to hear about these groups several times before they catch on that the object is not sermon critiques. It might be helpful when starting the process to tie it to a larger planning process or to a theme for the coming year and to outline that bigger picture for the congregation. The oversight group should remind participants that they are not expected to do a critique or an evaluation but simply to let church leaders know what they have experienced in certain programs—feedback that is essential if the church's mission and ministry are to be carried out effectively by the congregation. It is crucial not to signal inadvertently that something is wrong and needs to be fixed, when such is not the case. Make sure it is clear to everyone that this activity is not a one-time response to a problem but rather an ongoing approach to gathering regular feedback about various aspects of the church's life. Explain that sooner or later, most people in the church will be invited to participate in a feedback/reflection group related to a group, ministry, or activity that they have been part of. It would be useful to conduct some forums about habits of healthy communication and how they are practiced in these groups (teach the principles and give people opportunities to practice them).

The oversight team should explain to the congregation that feedback/reflection groups are not intended to make decisions or to solve problems. Any concerns, issues, problems, or new ideas will be directed to the appropriate officer or body—either to the ministerial staff or to the relevant church board or committee for problem-solving or planning for something new. When boards or committees become their own feedback/reflection groups, they may be the best ones to resolve issues or develop plans that they themselves identify. Even then, in the interest of keeping congregational leaders informed, boards or committees should report to the congregation's governing body the questions, issues, and actions that emerged from a committee holding its own feedback/reflection session.

3. Discerning What the Feedback Means

Immediately after a feedback/reflection group, the leader and the recorder report to the oversight group, which in turn asks whether anything has emerged from the group that needs attention soon. Does something need fixing right away by the minister, the trustees, the deacons, or the custodian? Is a revolt brewing because the minister makes offhand wisecracks while leading worship? Do the trustees need to make sure someone puts ice remover on the front walk before people show up for worship on Sundays? Is there a member needing pastoral care?

I know of one feedback/reflection group on the experience of worship in which a participant disclosed some difficult personal issues. She spoke in response to the question "Did you arrive for worship with any aches in your soul, and did something happen in worship that spoke to those aches?" This woman seized the opportunity to speak of the profound (and previously undisclosed) aches in her soul that morning as well as most other mornings. Fortunately, the minister was present. He had not been aware of this woman's pain, but responded helpfully in the session and followed up with her later. If the minister had not been present, the discussion leader would have asked, "May I share what you have told us with our minister?" An unplanned but important benefit for that participant was that several members of the group found their own ways to offer gentle support to her.

The oversight group and the minister should meet as needed to discuss the reports of recent feedback/reflection sessions. This group needs to ask:

- What are we learning?
- Are we getting clear information from the sessions, or are we getting ambiguous messages that we can't easily interpret?
- Has anything surprising emerged that we need to pay attention to sooner rather than later (or not at all)?
- Does anything we have heard suggest a need for us to adjust the kinds of feedback/reflection groups we plan to organize or the questions we plan to ask in the sessions already in the works?
- Who needs to receive what we have learned and when do they need to hear from us?

4. Reporting Findings

In keeping with the criterion of timeliness, it is important that the oversight group promptly report what it is learning from the feedback/reflection groups to those who need to know. In addition, boards and committees that have functioned as their own feedback/reflection groups should report what they have learned about themselves and about how the minister works with them, along with any adjustments they have made. Their report should go to the governing body soon after they have held their feedback/reflection sessions.

At least once a year, a summary of what has been learned in the feedback/reflection groups needs to be reported by the oversight group to the governing body and the congregation. This report should include:

1. A summary of what was learned about people's experiences in the areas of congregational life that were the focus of the groups this past year.
2. A report on what was done with pressing concerns, if any.
3. An assessment of issues, challenges, and opportunities before this congregation as these have emerged from the feedback/reflection groups, especially as they affect our understanding of our mission, vision, and sense of identity.
4. Input from ministerial staff people about their interpretation of the information, and, as appropriate, discussion of goals that the staff may have prepared in response to this information. If the congregation has a planning cycle that includes asking the minister for recommendations for congregational goals, it might be helpful for the minister to draw on information learned from the feedback/reflection groups for making goal recommendations. Others could also use the information gathered for their goal setting.

In addition to such a report from the oversight group to the governing body and the congregation, any group that has received feedback from a feedback/reflection group (or has held its own feedback/reflection session) may incorporate what it has learned into its annual report to the congregation:

As a result of our feedback/reflection group, we learned _____, _____, and _____ about ourselves. We have taken this information into account as we made our plans for next year and have established these goals for ourselves: _____, _____, and _____.

Chapter 6 gives a more detailed example of how this report was handled in one church.

5. Assimilating Results into Congregational Life

The payoff of the "Completing the Circle" process is a stronger congregational mission and ministry. When the process works well, relationships between members are strengthened, and leadership can lead more effectively by knowing how to ask for and receive high-quality feedback. Most important, planning for mission and ministry can take into account the reliable and valid feedback that flows to those who lead. New opportunities become known, tough issues become better understood, and annoying diversions can be avoided.

From time to time thus far I have alluded to how "Completing the Circle" might be an important resource for a congregation's planning cycle. Any such process worth considering includes a phase often referred to as evaluation or self-assessment. The core question is based on who we believe ourselves to be and what we believe our mission to be. How are we doing? In other words, what parts of our mission to we carry out really well? Where do we stumble? How well does our staff help us accomplish our mission? Assuming that we are not satisfied with staying the same, how can we fulfill God's call to us more effectively?

Although "Completing the Circle" is not designed to be a complete congregational planning process, it will, when used well, provide an abundance of helpful information for a larger planning process. Even if no larger planning process is under way, it is still important to channel what is learned from feedback/reflection groups into the ongoing life of the congregation. This feedback may result in major changes or only in minor adjustments. Changes, big or small, should be made in accordance with the polity of the congregation. In the interest of letting congregation members know that the "Completing the Circle" process has had a beneficial impact on their congregation, the oversight group should report to the congregation what has happened as a result of members' participation in feedback/reflection groups. Always begin and end such reports with a resounding "Thanks!" to all participants.

Frequently Asked Questions

Q: *What about group leaders? Does being a discussion leader take so much specialized training that we should hire people for the task? If we provide our own, how do we find them and train them?*
A: Good leaders are necessary for this process to work well, so it is a good idea for the oversight group to think carefully about whom it will ask to serve. Most congregations have members who seem gifted at eliciting discussion from group members without imposing their own opinions. Such individuals are also good at keeping a group on track. Thus, it is usually not necessary to look outside the congregation.

The oversight group should consider offering a training event for discussion leaders. The trainees should become familiar with the entire "Completing the Circle" process. They should learn the habits of healthy communication in the parish and should study carefully the suggested discussion guide for the sessions they will oversee. If a group is available, conveners-in-training might find it useful to participate in a feedback/reflection session led by someone else.

When I have led feedback/reflection groups, these have been my biggest challenges:

1. helping people to stay focused on describing their experiences rather than on making evaluative comments;
2. keeping the group from trying to solve problems;
3. bringing the group back to the topic *for that group* after a few people start chasing another topic; and
4. making sure every participant has a chance to respond to the questions.

I have always found that a gentle approach works well in bringing the group back from such detours. I have never needed to behave like a drill sergeant.

Under no circumstances should the discussion leader use the feedback/reflection group as an opportunity to lobby a captive audience on any issue. When choosing candidates for this role, by all means avoid inviting people well known in the congregation for wanting to remove the ministers. Rather, select folk who are perceived to be fair, unbiased, good listeners. If a person bent on sowing dissension served as group leader, those who shared his or her sentiments about the minister might look upon feedback/reflection groups as an arena for pursuing their agenda. Others, by contrast, might be leery of the process and refuse to be part of it.

Q: *Should our minister be present for feedback/reflection groups? Won't the presence of the pastor inhibit some people from saying what they really think?*
A: The "Completing the Circle" process is intended to be an example of healthy communication in the congregation. One of the marks of healthy communication is that people are encouraged to say what they need to say to those who need to hear it. Thus, it makes little sense to exclude the minister on the premise that people will feel freer to talk about him or her.

As often as possible, ministerial staff should be present for these groups—mostly to listen but also to ask clarifying questions, an important listening skill. It is one of many ways to encourage participants to tell their own story and make sure that others understand it as the speaker intended. The ministerial staff can also let participants know which board, committee, or person will take up concerns or questions raised in the session.

A feedback/reflection group does not offer a chance for ministers to elaborate on what they were trying to accomplish in last Sunday's sermon or to defend a program or a sermon that didn't go well. However, it may be appropriate and useful for ministerial staff to ask specific questions about issues that are not referred to in the discussion guides. For example, in one church where I had introduced this process, worshipers appeared increasingly to feel that the time of the offering during the service had lost its power as a meaningful act of worship. With many people mailing in pledge payments monthly, or making use of automatic withdrawals, or meeting a pledge with a one-time gift of appreciated stock at the end of the year, fewer and fewer people were putting money in the offering plate during Sunday worship. The deacons had asked themselves, "How can we reclaim the offering as an act of worship?" When feedback/reflection groups met to talk about what participants experienced in worship, the minister, on behalf of the deacons' board, asked, "What was your experience of the offering this morning?" The answers confirmed the suspicions of the minister and the deacons:

"I was embarrassed when I put nothing in the plate, even though my pledge was not only up-to-date but even paid ahead."

"It was basically an empty moment for me. My mind wandered all over the place."

"I enjoyed the music, but that's all there was to it. I could have enjoyed the same music at any other time in the service."

"Did I have a sense of this being an act of gratitude to God for all of God's blessings to us and to me, specifically? No, even though I know in my head that this is what I am supposed to do during the offering."

One person reported that out of a sense of duty, she disciplined herself to say a silent prayer of thanks, even though she did not put anything in the plate. As she said, "I knew I should do something like say a prayer of thanks. But I did not feel especially thankful in the depths of my heart."

Because the deacons had asked for this feedback, it was important to report to them promptly. No deacon was available to sit in on that feedback/reflection session, so the deacons asked the minister to report back to them. The minister, the leader, and the recorder met briefly after that session to be sure they had all heard the same information. Once they were satisfied that they had received the same feedback, the minister reported the findings to the full board of deacons. This feedback confirmed for the deacons the need for them and their minister to think together about ways to reclaim the joy of thankful giving as an act of worship. This feedback/reflection group did not itself provide a solution, nor was it supposed to. But the feedback helped the deacons and the minister realize that the loss of meaning of the Sunday offering was greater than they had imagined it might be.

Q: *What if the feedback/reflection groups reveal pockets of great unhappiness with our minister? What do we do with that?*
A: First, individual members of the oversight group should resist the temptation to step outside the process to seek corroborating information on their own. As soon as it becomes known that one or more members of the oversight group are talking with members of the congregation and asking whether

they have ever been unhappy with the minister, a host of un-pleasant reactions may follow.

"They are trying to get rid of our minister!"

"Let me tell you what that minister did to me and my family!"

"So that's why pledges are down. I wonder what else they will find."

The oversight group should also resist the temptation to tell the minister it is time for her or him to leave. That goes beyond what a "Completing the Circle" oversight team should do. But it would be a good idea for the oversight team to meet with the minister to try to make sense of this negative feedback. Then the team should report the troubling feedback to the governing body, along with its own assessment about what the responses mean. In the interest of healthy communication, I believe the minister should be present when this report is made.

The governing body may consider inviting in a consult-ant—an association or conference minister or other judica-tory staff member, or a consultant skilled in conflict education and mediation—to work with appropriate lay leaders and the minister. They should seek to develop a strategy for hearing the concerns and responding to them in a manner that will most likely foster the well-being of the church and its mission and ministry.

A plan may include direct meetings with those who have ex-pressed unhappiness, the minister, and at least one lay leader to hear and understand the concerns. After those meetings, the min-ister and the appropriate lay leaders will develop a plan to address the complaints. In the midst of all this, private counsel between the association or conference minister and the congregation's minister should take place to examine the full range of faithful responses. Judicatory staff might need to meet with one or two key lay leaders, too.

Q: *If this process is supposed to embody habits of healthy commu-nication, how will people know what those habits are?*
A: Some churches I work with have the practice of preparing a big chart, posting it where everyone can see it, and listing habits of healthy communication. The items are frequently referred to at the beginning of church meetings as a reminder to everyone about the kind of communication expected in this

meeting. Sometimes these charts have a series of "I statements," such as:

- I tell my own story and let others tell theirs.
- I avoid "awfulizing" negative experiences.
- I say what needs to be said to the one who needs to hear it.
- I devote at least as much energy to careful listening as to careful speaking.
- If something prompts anger in me, I report it honestly in a way that invites positive solutions.
- I refrain from blaming and shaming.

Q: *What if we have lots of people who don't like to disclose many personal things about themselves, such as their deepest religious feelings (or the lack thereof)? Doesn't this process depend on self-disclosure?*

A: Participants in feedback/reflection groups should be encouraged to say as much or as little as they are comfortable with. These groups are not for the purpose of spilling one's insides for all to see, although certainly there may be some very tender thoughts and feelings that are shared. Discussion leaders should do whatever it takes to help people feel safe in feedback/reflection groups. That also means that if a group member jumps on another group member, the leader may need to intervene to make sure that everyone feels emotionally and spiritually safe.

The leader may help people feel safe by inviting each feedback/reflection group to set its own ground rules. He or she asks participants to think about what they need to feel safe in the group. What they say is written on a flip chart (preferably verbatim, but if an entry needs to be edited for brevity or clarity, the person with the marking pen might ask, "May I write ___?"). Finally, the leader asks the group if these are rules they can live with. He or she explains that the rules belong to the participants— and that they (not the leaders) are the ones responsible for making sure they are followed.

Q: *Will the dominant racial/ethnic makeup of the congregation be a factor in how well this process works?*

A: Possibly. The work of Virstan Choy on the differences between Asian American congregations and Euro-American congregations in managing church conflict suggests that certain cultural values and norms influence interpersonal communication in congregations. Choy says that Asian American congregations tend to have a greater sensitivity to these factors than do most Euro-American congregations:

- the power of the relational orientation (that is, the conviction that preserving relationships is more important than solving disputes);
- the predisposition toward preserving relationship;
- the preference for nonconfrontational interaction; and
- the paradox of solidarity in the midst of conflict[1] (the notion that we are unified even when we disagree).

Choy says that because Asian American congregations tend to have a greater sensitivity to these factors, conflict resolution techniques based on confrontation and a considerable degree of self-disclosure will usually not succeed in Asian American congregations.

If the "Completing the Circle" process required confrontation and extensive self-disclosure, then we might notice reluctance to use it in congregations (Asian American or otherwise) that observe the norm of preserving relationships at all costs. Confrontation and extensive self-disclosure might come about in this process, but such a style is not required to make the process work.

Q: *What might cause this process to fail?*
A: Several factors might cause this process to go nowhere. A highly defensive minister who becomes angry with anyone describing an incident or action hinting that he or she has not measured up will send the process awry. Imagine that Joe says during a worship feedback/reflection group, "When the sermon was about half over, my mind drifted away to last summer's canoe trip. I didn't come back to church until all of a sudden we were standing up singing the Doxology." If the minister or another group member takes aim at Joe for his inattention, the circle of communication will not be completed. Joe gave honest feedback, but he paid a price for doing so. Such dynamics take a toll on this process!

If a church holds only one feedback/reflection group and thinks it has done the whole process, that church may miss the benefits of conducting several groups in more than one area of congregational life. I have worked, however, with several churches where so far only one group has met. The ministers reported that they received more feedback in that one hour than they had heard in all their previous years of service. This experience tells me that great value can accrue from holding only one feedback/reflection group, even if the full process can't be completed at this time. A congregation and its minister can also benefit from holding several groups focused only on one part of the congregation's life. A congregation may want to know more about what has drawn new members into the congregation in recent years, and what has worked or hasn't worked in retaining those members. Good information might be derived from a single feedback/reflection group to which all new members are invited who have come to the congregation during the last two years.

If a church is in the grip of major conflict, it will be difficult, and perhaps harmful, to begin this process. If serious tensions obtain between minister and congregation, I urge de-escalation efforts with the help of a consultant before embarking on the process.

If a congregation has developed habits of unhealthy communication over its lifetime, this process may not be an instant success. It takes effort and energy to learn new patterns of communication. Some folk try but wear out and abandon the effort. Some never try because the risks are too great. After all, how we communicate is inextricably woven into how we relate to one another. Thus, to change patterns of communication almost guarantees changes in patterns of relating, which in turn may raise anxiety about some of our most important relationships. In such circumstances, it is highly unlikely that the full "Completing the Circle" process will take hold. In such a setting, the wise minister will move forward in small steps and be grateful for whatever high-quality feedback comes to him or her. This might mean gradually teaching habits of healthy communication—by modeling, by holding classes (perhaps about "unrelated" subjects, such as how teens and parents can get along better), by teaching various groups and committees how to set and monitor ground rules, and so forth.

There you have the whole process, with one exception. Chapter 4 contains a collection of suggested discussion guides, all of which should be modified to fit your circumstances. Then chapters 5 and 6 bring us back to Sand Lake United Church of Christ, where we will see how one local congregation put everything in this chapter into practice.

NOTE

1. Virstan Choy, "From Surgery to Acupuncture: An Alternative Approach to Managing Curch Conflict from an Asian American Perspective," *Congregations* (Bethesda, Md.: Alban Institute): Nov/Dec 1995, 16–19.

Sample Discussion Guides for Feedback/Reflection Groups

Every group should begin with a few moments of connecting. At the most basic level, make sure that everyone has met everyone else. Because of time limitations it may be tempting to skip introductions or check-ins. If someone comes to the group with a heavy heart over a concern unrelated to the purpose of the group, it is likely that that person's pain will be expressed somehow in the discussion. The discussion leader should ask for introductions and should give people opportunity for brief check-ins, perhaps sharing with the group their current life concerns. Then the leader may offer a brief prayer. If a pressing concern was named during the check-in time, the prayer should place that concern in God's loving care. The prayer should also ask for God's Spirit to be in and among our conversation, and that this time together may be a blessing for our congregation.

After the prayer, the leader may want to do these things:

- Review with the group the chart listing healthy habits of communication that we encourage in this process.
- Review with the group the difference between evaluative feedback and descriptive feedback, reminding people that we are asking for descriptions of what they themselves have experienced in the aspect of congregational life that we are discussing in this session.
- Ask people if they would like to suggest ground rules for the group to follow, to help everyone feel comfortable. These should be noted on newsprint posted where everyone can see the list.

It would be easy to let time slip away with these opening steps. If the group is willing to allow an hour and a half for the session, the introductory exercises might be allotted as much as half an hour. If people are expecting to be done with the meeting in an hour, try to keep the opening steps to a maximum of 15 minutes.

Responding to Surprises

The guides on the following pages are only examples. The value of this process will be enhanced if leaders and the pastor (and perhaps other staff, board members, committee chairs and members, depending on the focus of the review) spend time reviewing the sample questions. They should ask:

- What do we want and need to know in our setting?
- What are the particular questions related to *our* congregation?
- What decisions are we preparing to make related to this review?
- What do we need to know before making those decisions?

Don't be afraid to experiment with the questions you ask. You may be surprised at what people tell you. When I first developed the sample questions about the experience of worship, I almost discarded the first one, "What was it like for you preparing to come to worship this morning?" But I left it in for the first group I led and was stunned at the response. After a moment of silence, one young woman said, "Well, it was hell for me. I have three children, as you know, and get no help, none whatsoever, from my husband. It was a battle from the minute the sun came up, and we were late getting here despite my efforts. I don't know if people really stared at us as we walked in late, or if it was just my imagination. But I felt judged when I walked in with crabby kids who still had Cheerios stuck to their clothes. I took my place during the Prayer of Confession and instead of praying what everyone else was praying, I said, 'You know what, God? There had darn well better be something worth this effort this morning!'"

The rest of the group was silent. Then someone gently asked, "And was there?"

The woman paused and nodded a "yes."

Someone else asked, "What was it?"

She said, "This moment. Right now. This very moment. This is the first time I have felt loved in a long time."

Spontaneously, the group gathered around her and gave her a warm hug. Ten minutes later, group members sat back down and resumed the discussion. What a way to begin! Several weeks later, the minister said, "You know, I had never realized what an effort it was for her or for others like her to get to church. Since that morning, I have become far more sensitive to what some of our folk have to go through just to get here, and I am trying to reflect that sensitivity in the prayers and in our welcome. I want our welcome to worship to be genuine and to be itself a trans-forming experience."

I included that question not because I had any special insight or hunch about what people might say. But now whenever I lead a feedback/reflection group, that question stays in the discus-sion, and I am more aware than ever that we may be surprised.

As this experience shows, holy, life-transforming moments may happen in feedback/reflection groups. Be open to that possibility.

Discussing Our Experience of Worship

1. What was it like for you preparing to come to worship this morning?

2. Did you come with any particular aches in your soul, or any particular joys or reasons for thanksgiving? If so, was there any place or time when the service of worship connected with your aches or your joys?

3. The mystics of old sometimes said of worship, "This is where I fall in love with God all over again." Was there any time in the service when you were especially aware of the love of God?

4. About the sermon:
   A. What were the highlights for you?
   B. Did anything you heard challenge you?
   C. Did you find new insight? If so, what was the insight?
   D. Did you hear good news in it? If so, when?

5. About today's hymns: Did you sing them with gusto? Lose your place? Relish every word and note? Breathe a sigh or relief when we were done? Wish there were more verses? (Other questions or responses may be added.)

6. What did you experience during the offering?

7. Announcements: Were they welcoming and inviting? Did you know who was making them? Did you know whether you were welcome to come to the events that were announced?

8. How many of your senses were appealed to in today's service?

9. How about the pacing of this service? Did you stay up comfortably with the flow? Did you wish it would move along faster? Find yourself two steps behind? (Other questions may be added.)

10. How did you respond to today's choral music? To today's instrumental music?

11. Were there any parts of the service that were hard for you to follow? Any parts that made you wonder, "Why in the world do we do *this*?"

12. When we celebrate Holy Communion, what do you usually experience?
13. When we celebrate a baptism, what do you usually experience?
14. What else would you like to add about your experience of worship today?

Discussing our Experience
of Committee Membership

Hold this discussion about halfway through the year at a regular meeting of the committee. Limit conversation to about an hour so that other matters can be dealt with.

1. What do you have to do at work or home to be able to attend these meetings?
2. When you arrive for our meetings, what helps you engage fully in what the committee needs to do?
3. Do you experience anything that makes it difficult for you to carry out your duties as a faithful member of this committee? If so, what?
4. What things bring you satisfaction as a member of this committee?
5. Have you experienced any challenges—hard issues with few or no solutions—in your service on this committee? If so, have these been resolved?
6. What else would you like to say about your experience of being a member of this committee?

Being a Volunteer Church School Teacher or Youth Group Sponsor

Hold this discussion about halfway through a teaching cycle with people who are now serving in these positions. Youth group sponsors might hold this discussion about halfway through a program year. Depending on the number of volunteer leaders, this discussion may need to take place in smaller groups. If the group includes more than 10 people, the opportunity for in-depth discussion diminishes substantially. Because youth fellowship programs vary so widely, those responsible for these programs should review the questions below and add questions that fit their congregation.

1. Typically, what is it like for you to prepare for the sessions for which you are responsible?
2. What have been your most fulfilling experiences in this position thus far? What do you think has made these experiences so positive?
3. Do you experience anything that makes it hard for you to carry out your responsibilities for this position?
4. Have you dealt with any awful experiences in this position? If so, have those been resolved to your satisfaction?
5. What else would you like to say about your experience of being a volunteer teacher or leader for children or youth?

The Experience of Receiving Pastoral Care

Gather no more than 10 people (five or six might be more satis-factory) who have within the past year received pastoral care from the minister and the church following a death in the family, other major loss (job, property in natural disaster, divorce), or a seri-ous health crisis. Because of confidentiality issues, it may be best to invite only those whose crisis was known to the congregation (i.e., the kind of situation that is likely to be announced during "Joys and Concerns" in a worship service). The questions should be tailored to fit whatever systems are in place or that church members are considering putting in place. If a congregation has a Befriender program or a Stephen Ministry program, one may need to ask specifically about how those programs worked for group participants. Most congregations have some congregationally based capacity to respond to members in crisis. Obviously, the leader needs to make sure that participants feel safe and do not feel pressured to speak about anything they do not wish to dis-close. Because it is likely that the minister has shared intense moments with participants in the past and that these intense moments will be referred to in the discussion, participants may feel more at ease if the minister is the primary discussion leader.

Participants need to be reminded that the discussion is de-signed to help both the minister and others in the church ensure that the church's ministries with people in crisis are as effective as possible. Often, those who have experienced major crises have had needs that would far outstrip the capacity of any congrega-tion to respond to all of them. Participants should be reminded that this session does not imply promises about what the church will be able to do for its members in crisis. But the minister or a "care-giving" church member may be able to strengthen what the church now does in response to such needs.

1. As you feel comfortable speaking, would you de-scribe the journey you have been through? Would you especially talk about your contact with the church—our minister and other members of the congregation—during this experience?
2. What do you remember being among the most help-ful offers of help you experienced in your contact with the church?

3. Do you remember ever wishing that something different would happen in your contact with the church during this time? If so, what would that have been?
4. In the interests of helping our minister and our church do the very best job possible of being supportive to people in crisis, is there anything else you would like us to know about your own experiences?

The Experience of Being a New Member

Although it would be good to hear from all new members of the past five years, that would, for some churches, be an unwieldy number. I suggest gathering about 12 members who have joined the congregation in the past two years. If some have already become inactive, their participation, if they could be motivated to attend, might be revealing and helpful.

1. How did you happen to visit this church in the beginning?
2. What helped you to decide this was the church you wanted to join?
3. How easy or hard has it been for you to feel that you know what is going on in this church?
4. How easy or hard has it been for you to get to know other people in this congregation?
5. What programs or groups have you become part of, if any, and how easy or hard was it for you to become part of these programs or groups?
6. What has been the role of the pastor in helping you decide to join this church and in helping you settle in?
7. What has been the role of our members in helping you decide to join this congregation and helping you settle in?

Our Experience of Being Part of an Outreach Project

Gather about 10 people who have had recent experiences in some ministry beyond the local church. Depending on what information is desired and what decisions will be based on this feedback, the people invited may be ones who all participated in the same project or who participated in different outreach programs. Their feedback can help answer numerous questions: How does our church decide what projects to engage in? How well do we support our people who get involved? What kind of connection is there between our congregation and the projects some of our people engage in?

1. Please describe briefly what activity you were (or are) involved in beyond our local church.
2. How did you decide to get involved?
3. What sort of support and encouragement for your efforts do you experience from our church, either from members or from ministers? How might our congregation better support this effort?
4. Are there ways that you would like to share more fully with our congregation what you have experienced in ministries beyond the parish?

Being Part of an Educational Experience Led by Our Minister

1. Please describe the class or event and what motivated you to participate.
2. As far as you could tell, what were the primary objectives of this experience—to impart new information, to motivate participants to take some action, to help people explore their faith in God, to foster personal growth and self-understanding, to help people gain new skills in church leadership, or to help people strengthen their relationship with the church? (Other answers are also possible.)
3. Briefly, what was the subject content of this class?
4. What were the primary teaching methods used in this class? How did you experience those methods?
5. What, for you, is one central new idea, insight, piece of information, or new challenge that came from this class?

Checklist on Ministers and Mission

This checklist on the ministerial role in relation to the congregation's mission is not a discussion guide but rather an instrument to be used by lay leaders in assessing the organizational and resource support available to its staff and lay leaders. Any performance review of ministerial staff should be accompanied by an assessment of this nature. A check under the "yes" column means that the item is current and generally known in the congregation.

RESOURCE ASSESSMENT CHECKLIST

Item	Yes	No	Out of Date	Not Widely Known
1. Our congregation has vision and mission statements that provide ongoing guidance for what we do.				
2. Our congregation has a functioning constitution and by-laws that contain in broad outline our church's understanding of the role of our minister and members.				
3. Our congregation has current position descriptions for our ministerial staff.				
4. Our congregation has a planning cycle that includes setting goals, objectives, and priorities for the congregation and the ministerial staff.				
5. Our congregation expects progress on meeting goals, objectives, and priorities to be reported regularly to the governing body.				
6. Our congregation follows the practice of assessing regularly whether the ministerial staff, lay officers, and congregational committees have the resources to fulfill position descriptions and to meet goals, objectives, and priorities.				

Sand Lake UCC Embarks
on "Completing the Circle"

A few months after the personnel committee of Sand Lake United Church of Christ held the discussion reported in chapter 1, the committee, with the blessing and encouragement of the church council, decided to use the "Completing the Circle" approach to reviewing the ministries of the congregation. Here is what happened.

Making a List

Members of the personnel committee—Shelly, Dale, Mary, Fritz, and Marvin—met to make plans. Shelly, the committee chair, said, "Folks, I have been thinking that if we want to make this process work for us, we should take some time now rather than later to think about how we are going to run this thing."

"That makes good sense to me," said Fritz. "What if we generate a checklist of the things we need to do ahead of time, and then what we will do while we are running the feedback/reflection groups, and then what we will do after we have run a few groups? If we develop a checklist, we can be sure we know what needs to be done under each of the steps and we can be clear who will do it."

The personnel committee discussed what would need to be done for this congregation to make the process work well. After long discussion, they developed the outline of a checklist on a large sheet of newsprint. Dale offered to prepare a more detailed outline for the committee to use in its planning. Marvin agreed to edit Dale's draft. The following week, here is what they presented to the committee:

"COMPLETING THE CIRCLE" CHECKLIST

1. Inform the congregation about this process so that when people are invited to participate in a feedback/ reflection group, they will know what that is all about. We will emphasize that we are using this process as a healthy alternative to conducting performance evaluations of our ministers. We will especially emphasize the statement: *"Good feedback is to our community life what breathing and eating are to our biological lives. Without it, we simply do not function very well in community, no matter what the community."* We will stress that we are doing this work to enhance the health and effectiveness of our church life, and not because we think some terrible problem needs to be fixed.
   A. We will prepare and send a general letter to the congregation.
   B. We will prepare paragraphs as reminders for our newsletter and for the Sunday worship bulletin.
   C. We will prepare a one-page description of the process to give to new members in our membership classes.
   D. We will prepare and present occasional announcements for Sunday worship, both about specific feedback/reflection groups that are under way and about the process in general.

2. We will prepare ourselves to coordinate feedback/ reflection groups.
   A. We will ourselves participate in a feedback/reflection group on our own experience of worship—a group led by a consultant from our association or from a neighboring church that has used this process.
   B. We will assign two of our number to each group and determine that one committee member will lead while the other takes notes.

C. We will study the book *Completing the Circle* carefully, with special attention to the section on habits of healthy communication.

D. We will make a chart on "Habits of Healthy Communication" as found in the book, and begin each feedback/reflection group by reviewing these habits.

E. In our own committee work, we will make every effort to practice these habits of healthy communication so that they become second nature to us, and so that we ourselves may appropriately demonstrate these habits.

F. We will offer ourselves to the Christian education committee to lead at least three adult education forums on habits of healthy communication in the church. We will offer one forum each quarter, except for summer, and do all we can to encourage members to attend at least once.

3. We will develop a plan for one year, listing what kinds of feedback/reflection groups are most needed and when they will be held.

A. We will ask for time at a church council meeting (at least 30 minutes) to explain the process and to solicit requests from various boards and committees as to which areas of our church life need the kind of attention that can be given through a feedback/reflection group. We assume that the council has final authority to determine which areas will be addressed first.

B. After hearing requests from boards and committees, we will develop our first-year plan with no more than 10 feedback/reflection groups the first year.

C. After our plan for the first year is established, we will publicize the plan to let the congregation know what we are doing.

D. Once we have developed our first-year plan, we will review the suggested discussion guides in *Completing the Circle*, and we will adjust and adapt the questions in the discussion guides to fit our church. Our ministers need to be involved in this part of the process so that the questions we ask in the feedback/reflection groups provide us with the most useful, relevant information possible.

4. Once we have developed our plan for the first year, we will determine the best strategy for inviting people to participate.
   A. For groups discussing the experience of worship, we will create sign-up lists with 12 slots for each scheduled group. These sign-up lists will be circulated whenever people are together until all slots are filled. Two weeks before each group is to meet, one member of our committee will send a letter to those who signed up, reminding them of the time and the purpose. The sign-up lists will include a note letting people know that they will receive a reminder letter two weeks before the scheduled meeting.
   B. For groups on other aspects of our church life, we will decide whom to invite and how to invite them once we know what parts of our church life we will be focusing on.

5. We will follow up on each feedback/reflection group in these ways:
   A. The committee member assigned to take notes will prepare a brief, legible summary of the meeting for our own files, which we will first review with our ministers after the meeting.
   B. Both committee members assigned to a group will ask themselves: Are there issues, concerns, or other feedback that should be given right away to someone, such as our ministers, lay leaders, or other staff? They will refer such matters by phone or e-mail in a timely manner.
   C. At least twice a year our committee will meet with our ministers and other staff to review feedback provided in the feedback/reflection groups. Our

ministers and other staff are expected to use this information for professional goal-setting. We will invite committee chairs and other lay leaders to take feedback to their committees and set goals incorporating what they've heard, as appropriate. We will ask our ministers and other staff to incorporate their professional goals in their annual written reports to the congregation, and in future years, to include in the reports progress on the previous year's goals.

Preparing for the Feedback Groups

"Wow," said Mary. "This is quite a task. Are you sure we are up to it?"

"Absolutely," said Fritz. "Yes, there is a lot to do here, but when I compare this work to the frustration that comes from running those old performance reviews, I like this style. Given how important healthy interpersonal communication is for the well-being of a church, you would think that paying attention to getting reliable feedback would be routine. But, of course, that isn't the case. I understand that our ministers and the members who have learned about this venture are actually looking forward to it because they believe it will give them a much better idea of how things are really going for the church. If we do this process well, our ministers, other staff, and lay leaders, including the council, are going to get a lot more high-quality feedback than anything that ever came to them either from keeping their ears to the ground or from reading our old evaluation questionnaires."

Shelly said, "To get us moving, what if we think out loud together about how we are going to present this process so we can be sure that we say what needs to be said? I would be glad to draft what I think we have said and ask for your responses."

"You mean you think we should give you high-quality feedback about what you are doing?" asked Dale.

"You betcha," Shelly said with a laugh. "Then after we have done that, I will go to the church council to talk about this process and ask council members for their ideas about what aspects of our church life we should review this first year."

Committee members suggested various pieces of the process that needed to be explained while Shelly took careful notes. After they adjourned, she drafted the documents that follow. When they reconvened, they reviewed what she had drafted, and finally agreed on these documents:

1. A LETTER INTRODUCING THE PROCESS TO THE CONGREGATION

Dear friends,

We are writing as members of the personnel committee of Sand Lake United Church of Christ about an exciting new process we have decided to use in our congregation to help provide high-quality feedback to our ministers, other staff, and lay leaders about how our members are experiencing the life and mission of our church.

In years past, we conducted annual performance evaluations of our ministers. Well, they were supposed to be annual, but often we didn't get it done each year. For many reasons, we have never been confident in the quality of information provided by that performance evaluation. We have decided this year to start using a simple but quite different process called "Completing the Circle." Briefly, in this process small groups of our members will be invited to meet with two members of our personnel committee and, in some cases, with one or both of our ministers, in "feedback/reflection groups."

Feedback/reflection groups will provide an opportunity for participants to talk with one another about what they are experiencing in various aspects of our church's life and mission. A key feature here is that we will be asking people *not* to evaluate what they have experienced, but simply to share what the experience was like. This important aspect of the feedback/reflection groups will be explained in more detail at the beginning of each group.

Each feedback/reflection group will have a specific focus. In a few groups the discussion will center on what participants experience in our services of worship. Over time there will be groups that discuss the experience of being a member of one of our boards or committees. Others will discuss the experience of being a new member of our congregation. Other groups will focus on other aspects of our life and mission.

In a few more weeks, after our personnel committee has developed a schedule for the coming year, more information will be coming to you about when and how you will be asked to participate in a feedback/reflection group. We can tell you now that for groups that will discuss the experience of worship, we will be circulating sign-up lists for several dates, and you will be invited to sign up for one group during the coming year.

We want to emphasize that we are initiating this method *not* in response to a problem in our congregation. We want to put into place an easy system for obtaining high-quality feedback, and we want that system to rely on healthy habits of interpersonal communication. We believe that *good feedback is to our community life what breathing and eating are to our biological lives. Without it, we simply do not function very well in community, no matter what the community.*

You will be hearing lots more about this process. Don't hesitate to call any member of the personnel committee if you have questions or concerns.

Sincerely,
[Committee members' names and phone numbers]

2. SAMPLE PARAGRAPHS FOR WORSHIP BULLETIN OR CHURCH NEWSLETTER

GIVE US A PIECE OF YOUR MIND—AND HEART AND SOUL!

Feedback/reflection groups help our church complete the circle of communication. Feedback/reflection groups focusing on the experience of worship are now being organized. You may sign up for one such group (one meeting only!) on the sign-up lists that will be circulating around Fellowship Hall during coffee hour following worship the next two Sundays. Or you can call the church office or one of the members of our personnel committee, whose names are listed below. *Good feedback is to our community life what breathing and eating are to our biological lives!*

For further information, call the chair of our personnel committee, Shelly Martin, *[phone number]*.

• • • •

DID YOUR SPIRIT SING OR SLUMBER THE FIRST TIME YOU WALKED INTO SAND LAKE UNITED CHURCH OF CHRIST?

Feedback/reflection groups help our church complete the circle of communication. A feedback/reflection group focusing on the experience of being a new member of our congregation is now being organized. If you became a member of our church during the past two years, you will be invited by letter and by a phone call. This group will meet _____. Sharing your experience will help us strengthen our ability to be a welcoming, inviting congregation. *Good feedback is to our community life what breathing and eating are to our biological lives!*

For further information, contact the chair of our personnel committee, Shelly Martin, *[phone number]*.

• • • •

MY, HOW YOU'VE GROWN! TELL US ABOUT IT!

Feedback/reflection groups help our church complete the circle of communication. A feedback/reflection group is being organized on the experience of participating in an adult education class taught by our ministers. If you attended any of the adult education classes taught or led by our ministers during the past two years, we would very much like you to come to this group. We will be posting a sign-up list outside the church office, or you can call the office to sign up. The group will meet _____ for no more than an hour and a half, probably less. Because many people have attended an adult ed class, we will also be circulating a sign-up list during fellowship hour after worship for the next two Sundays. *Good feedback is to our community life what breathing and eating are to our biological lives!*

For further information, please call the chair of our personnel committee, Shelly Martin, *[phone number]*.

3. A DESCRIPTION OF THE PROCESS

This document will be given to new members as part of their orientation to this congregation, and to current members through the church newsletter:

HOW SAND LAKE COMPLETES THE CIRCLE

At Sand Lake United Church of Christ, we believe that it is important for the health of our congregation for us to communicate well with each other. One important component of good interpersonal communication is providing reliable feedback to our ministers, our other staff, and our lay leaders about how we are experiencing the life and mission of our church.

We have adopted a process called "Completing the Circle." We seek to complete the circle of communication by providing high-quality feedback to our leaders, which helps them know what is working well and what needs adjustment. Throughout the year, we convene small groups of our members in "feedback/reflection groups." These groups focus on a specific aspect of our church's life and mission. Using a discussion guide, a member of our personnel committee leads the groups, asking participants to talk about their own experience in that part of our church life. Another member of our personnel committee will take notes. If any of the concerns mentioned need attention right away, they will be referred to the appropriate people. About twice a year, the personnel committee and our ministers, other staff, and lay leaders meet to review what they have heard in these groups. Information provided in feedback/reflection groups becomes a vital resource as staff establish professional goals and lay leaders develop congregational goals.

What in the world are feedback/reflection groups? Is that in the Bible somewhere? Participants in feedback/reflection groups give *feedback* after *reflecting* on their own experiences in certain areas of our congregational life. Participants in feedback/reflection groups are identified in several ways, depending on the focus of the group. On an ongoing basis, we will have groups reflecting on the experience of worship. When we have these groups scheduled, we will circulate sign-up lists throughout the church community (such as during fellowship time after worship, or at church dinners). Or you can call the church office to sign up. For other groups, whose focus is on a specific aspect of our church life, we will invite members who have participated in that specific program to come to a feedback/reflection group.

We encourage participants to observe these guidelines:

1. Everyone's input is equally important. Each of us is an expert on our own experience. For example, we all experience *something* when we are together for worship, even if some may have been thinking about lunch instead of the sermon!

2. We do not try to outdo one another in showing how much we know about the topic we are discussing.

3. We discourage reporting of secondhand information and encourage people to tell their own stories.

4. We look for comments that *describe your own experiences*. For example, if you are part of a feedback/reflection group on worship, we look for such comments as, "When our minister said, '*x, y, and z*' in the sermon, I thought about a time when . . ." Or "When the choir sang the anthem, I felt _____." We are *not* asking you to evaluate what happened. We don't ask whether the sermon was a good sermon or a bad sermon, or whether the prayer was good or bad. We avoid *shoulds* and *oughts*, such as "We should have three services and fill them all up." But it is all right to report, "Gosh, it was lonely up there in that front pew all alone. . ."

5. We encourage attentive listening to one another. Listening to one another about what matters to the other person is as important as speaking about what matters to you.

6. Problem-solving is not our primary purpose in these groups. If something is raised that needs to be examined, we encourage honesty in a spirit of Christian love. The facilitator will make note of the concern for discussion and problem-solving at another time by the appropriate person or group.

Not only do we believe that this process will help us strengthen the ongoing ministry and mission that we carry out together in and through our church; we also believe that these groups enrich our relationships with one another.

Our feedback/reflection groups seek to embody a culture of healthy interpersonal communication. Habits of healthy communication include:

- I tell my own story and let others tell theirs.
- I avoid "awfulizing" negative experiences.
- I say what needs to be said to the one who needs to hear it.
- I devote as much energy to careful listening as to careful speaking.
- If something prompts anger in me, I report honestly how I feel in a way that invites positive solutions.
- I refrain from blaming and shaming.

It is important to us that these feedback/reflection groups be an example of healthy, loving communication worthy of the Body of Christ. We have come to realize that what we say and how we say it to one another has an impact on the whole Body of Christ.

For further information, please contact any member of the personnel committee: [names and phone numbers of committee]

LETTER TO PEOPLE WHO SIGNED UP FOR
A FEEDBACK/REFLECTION GROUP ON WORSHIP:

Thank you very much for signing up to participate in a feedback/ reflection group about the experience of worship. The group for which you signed up will meet on _____ in room _____. Your input is important to this process, so please call [name and phone number] right away if you are not able to come. This courtesy will allow us to invite someone else to this session and to help you find a time that will work better for you. Thanks! Also, if child care is essential to enable you to attend, please let us know.

Enclosed is a longer description of our process and the reasons behind it. We urge you to review this paper before coming. Thanks! (The same brochure that was prepared for new members will also be enclosed.)

Meeting with the Council

The personnel committee agreed that these various written statements explained the process well and would serve to recruit participants, although after seeing how people responded, the committee might need to rework what was prepared so far.

The next step was for Shelly to attend a meeting of the church council, which she did as soon as there was time available on the agenda. The evening after the meeting, she reported to the personnel committee the results of her visit.

"I attended the church council last night," said Shelly, "and explained to council members how feedback/reflection groups work. I reminded them that first, we understood this to be a much better alternative to our old hit-and-miss performance evaluations of our ministers. Then, second, that we were not using this process because we think there is some big problem between the congregation and our ministers. And third, that we really want to emphasize the value of getting reliable feedback for effective functioning of our staff and of council members as lay leaders. I then told them that we would like to establish a plan for the next year that would include at least six and no more than ten feedback/reflection groups. We wanted the council's help in deciding which areas of our life as a church should be our focus. Right away the deacons' representative said we should be sure to have several feedback/reflection groups on the experience of worship. When I told the council that we were already thinking we would have at least four sessions on worship, the members said immediately, 'Go for it.'

"For a whole lot of reasons, the Christian ed chair said we could wait until next year before doing more on Christian education. That was a long and sort of boring discussion, so I hope you'll take my word for it."

"That's a relief," said Fritz. "I had visions of every segment of the church wanting us to run four or five groups this next year. That would mean about two groups a week!"

"Not to worry," said Shelly. "We have wound up with requests for a total of eight for the year. That's one every other month plus two more. I want to do this often enough so that it does what we want the process to do, although since we haven't done this before, I am not sure how often that needs to be. Let's do this and then see next year whether it was too much or not enough."

"So four groups on worship," said Mary. "What are the other four?"

Shelly said, "One will focus on the experience of being a new member. Our evangelism and church growth committee has been doing some number-crunching, and has discovered that when someone joins this church, there is a greater than 50 percent chance that within two years, that person either will have stopped coming or will have officially withdrawn from membership. The evangelism and church growth folk think it is time to find out why the dropout rate is that high.

Their suggestion is that we try to include some of the drop-outs in this group, if they are willing to come."

"This is a really good idea," said Fritz. "I tend not to be connected to many of the grapevines in our church, but in this area I do hear some stuff. Apparently, the evangelism committee has mentioned those statistics aloud here and there, and I know of at least one person who latched onto that finding like a pit bull and is blaming our ministers for not doing a better job of retaining and integrating new members. I said to that person that maybe the real reason people dropped out is that they didn't like hearing long-term members complain about our ministers. But more to the point, the dropout rate of new members may be related to something Charlie and Susan are doing or not doing. But it may have even more to do with something the lay members are doing or not doing. And it could be that the reasons for these dropouts have nothing to do with anything we can change or control. This issue is worth looking at."

Shelly went on, "Then the next request came from the council itself, with strong support from the nominating committee—for a group focused on the experience of being a member of the church council. Our ministers said that one of their requests would dovetail here because they both would like better feedback about their role with the council. They said last night that they are not sure sometimes whether they should take a more active role in advocating for positions and programs, or whether they do that too much as it is. So the council and the ministers hope to strengthen their working relationship by getting reliable feedback from current and past council members.

"Then, after I was thinking that Christian education wouldn't need a group this year, Charlie said, 'What about confirmation?' Attendance hasn't been the greatest this year, and Charlie has heard indirect grumbling from some kids that some of the other kids are so rowdy that no one learns anything. So the council said that maybe we ought to include a group on confirmation, and, in fact, asked if we would be willing to run one with current class members and their parents and another with past class members and parents. So that will actually count as two when it comes to adding up the number of groups we will have."

Responding to Grief

Dale asked, "Were there other areas that will be deferred to another year?"

"Yes," said Shelly. "Reverend Charlie and Reverend Susan both said that they think we should take a hard look at how our church does ministry with people who have had a death in the family, or who have suffered some other major loss. We tend to do a pretty good job right away, but when the reality hits the bereaved a week or a month or six months later, we are kind of like the culture at large. We disappear. Charlie and Susan know that there are some predictable times when they as pastors should plan to make contact, but they would like to get a better idea about what the most useful action would be for the church to take. They have wondered about one of the formal programs of member care such as Befrienders. Do we have a need for something like that or some other organized response? Individual needs may be so different that we can't do any better than we now do. But Charlie and Susan say they are are feeling strongly that we don't have a good handle on this matter and that we won't until we hear from some of our own people about their experiences. And the pastors want to know whether this is an issue they should address alone or whether they need to organize some better response from the church. So next year, we will think carefully about how to invite folk who have had a major loss to participate in a conversation about their experience. This invitation will be awfully sensitive, but the council felt that if we gave ourselves time to think about how to do it, such a conversation could be a rich experience. After all, how often do people ever have a chance to tell others what their grief is really like, with particular attention to the issue of how their faith and their church did and did not help? If we knew ahead of time for sure what we will learn, we wouldn't need to do it!"

Mary said, "I think we are in for a grand experience here. Even though we won't look at many aspects of our church life this year, I think we will learn a lot. Many of our other leaders and Reverend Susan and Reverend Charlie will learn a whole lot more about how we experience their work here than they have ever learned previously. Let's finish carrying out the rest of our checklist and make this happen!"

Sand Lake Church, a Year and a Half Later

A few months after the personnel committee of Sand Lake United Church of Christ held the discussion reported in chapter 1, the personnel committee decided, with the blessing and encouragement of the church council, to use the approach described in this book to review the ministries of the congregation. A year and a half after that initial meeting, the church council met with the personnel committee, their agenda centering on the presentation of the annual report.

Shelly, chair of the personnel committee, began. "First, let me thank you for your encouragement to us to use the 'Completing the Circle' approach to reviewing the ministries of Sand Lake United Church of Christ. As you can tell from the way I phrased the extent of our work, we have done more than just evaluate the performance of our ordained ministers, Reverend Charlie and Reverend Susan. To be sure, we had plenty of opportunities to hear and learn about their work, but we also learned much that we know will be useful to the other staff and lay leaders of this church. The personnel committee was given the oversight role for this process because using this method evolved from our first trying to figure out how to conduct a fair and reasonable performance evaluation of our ministers. The pastoral relations committee might have done it just as well, and in the future, we should talk about handing this responsibility off to that committee.

Shelly and Dale then reviewed the committee's process, as described in chapter 5. Then it was Mary's turn to talk about what they had learned.

But before Mary could speak, the moderator asked, "Did you have people who didn't want to come to these groups, and did they tell you why?"

"Oh, sure," said Dale. "Some didn't have time, some said they didn't like to speak out loud in groups, and one person told me that what she experiences in worship is nobody's business but hers. People volunteered for the worship groups, but this woman heard my invitation, and, yes, I even asked her to consider coming, and that was her response. So, OK, this isn't meant to be unpleasant, and we decided it wasn't worth twisting anyone's arm. It took a lot of explaining for a lot of people. Many thought they were going to have to critique the minister's sermon or something like that. But once they heard what we were doing and why, they were glad to come. We promised everyone that groups like this will become a regular part of our life together, so we all learn from each other."

Mary began, "First, let me echo what Dale said about the spiritual benefit of doing this kind of review. Both from our recent meeting with just the personnel committee and then from leading other meetings, I have a much, much deeper sense of who we are as a faith community, and I like what I see.

"In our worship groups, we did learn some things right out of the chute that were frankly a little embarrassing, although no one meant them to be. The first thing is that we need to make large-print bulletins available every Sunday. We are generally a young congregation, and we have made some wrong assumptions about everyone's eyesight. In our very first group, one young woman, about 25 years old, told us that she could not participate in any of the printed litanies or prayers because she could not see them. She has a degenerative eye condition that none of us knew about. Reverend Charlie was in that group, and within a week, he saw to it that we were printing a dozen large-print bulletins each week. About 10 people are now using them regularly.

"Then our second group included a young father who spends most of his Sunday mornings with his infant son in the nursery behind the sanctuary. You know how some people at announcement time stand up and say, 'Oh, I don't need a microphone—everyone can hear me'? Well, not everyone can, especially those back in the nursery and the people using personal public-address systems (personal hearing aids that run through a public-address system). That's why you started seeing the notes in the bulletins and newsletter asking everyone to use the microphone for all announcements.

"On the whole, we heard over and over great appreciation for what happens in worship here. People report that they experience the love of God in many ways and places, but especially during baptisms and during communion. During baptisms, Reverend Charlie and Reverend Susan make sure that we know whom we are baptizing. They introduce the family members and put their names in the bulletin. So over and over people commented on how close they felt to the one being baptized and how they look forward to being around this child as he or she grows up in the church. Two people said that the experience of baptism is what led them to agree to teach church school.

"There were, besides all the upbeat responses, two concerns needing some attention, in our opinion; and both of these go way beyond the purview of the personnel committee. In fact, we're not sure who needs to address these areas, so that's why we bring them to you.

"One has to do with our worship music. Some folk love our music just the way it is, and told us quite clearly that they do not wish to see it tinkered with in any way. Others reported falling asleep, more or less—or at least wandering significantly—during most of our hymns. These folk expressed a yearning for more jazzy, bouncy hymns, easy to learn and easy to sing, but peppier than 12 verses of 'Just as I Am.'

"But even more pressing than the style of music is the issue of language in the hymn texts—specifically, gender-inclusive language versus language that contains lots of masculine images. Now clearly, we didn't need feedback/reflection groups to let most of us know that the texts of hymns is an issue around here, but these groups provided the first opportunity for respectful dialogue about it for many of our members. Several folk showed up ready to blame Reverend Charlie or Reverend Susan for choosing the wrong kinds of hymns; but fortunately, they backed off once they heard others talk about what they experienced with the hymns they love the most. So we lay the issue at the feet of our all-knowing church council, trusting that you will solve it for us by this time next week."

After the laughter subsided, Mary went on: "Let me name the other item needing attention, and this may or may not be an issue primarily for Reverend Charlie and Reverend Susan. You recall that the discussion guide includes a question to the effect, 'Did you come to worship today with any particular aches in your soul or joys in your heart, and was there any time in the service that connected with these aches or joys?' Fully 90 percent of those in the groups responded "yes" to the first part. Yes, they came with aches in their souls and joys in their hearts. But fewer than 10 percent said, 'Yes, there was some moment' in the service that connected to those aches or joys.' Then as people talked about hearing the sermon, they said in one way or another that the sermons are interesting, well delivered, well prepared, easy to follow . . . but just didn't seem to connect with what was happening in their lives all that often."

Reverend Susan said, "Since Charlie and I knew before tonight's meeting that this feedback was showing up, we have been thinking a lot about it, and it confirms something we have intuitively been feeling. That is, that all of us here at Sand Lake don't have very many opportunities to talk with each other around here about the important issues of the soul and questions of the heart and challenges to our life of faith. At least we hadn't until we started doing these feedback/reflections groups. So we have been wondering if now would be a good time to start offering small-group experiences a couple of times each week at different times so that people can get to one of them that would focus on the scripture lessons for the coming week. We would study the lessons, pray about them, examine our own lives to see what issues and questions get prompted in us by the scripture lessons and the like. Maybe this will help us connect more effectively."

Amber, chair of the deacons, responded, "I really like that idea. I would come, no doubt about it, and I would commit to inviting everyone I know who has ever said to me, 'Gosh, the sermons don't really fire me up very much.' What I like about this suggestion is that we have the chance here to respond as a community, and that will, we hope, keep us from picking at our ministers. I don't know for sure if much of that is going on, but let's head it off by doing something positive. We can't expect you to read our hearts and minds. Besides, I hope the eventual outcome will be to help us all be more faithful in our service as Christians in this world because we are better grounded spiritually."

"This is a really good idea," Mary responded, "and I hope that the council and our ministers will work out a plan like the one you have suggested. I think it is important to let the congregation know that you are putting this group together largely in response to what we have heard in the feedback/reflection groups, so that they can see some tangible results. But let me continue our report by telling you what we heard in the group of new members.

"About half of those who participated said it was hard for them to gain a sense of belonging. That's a significant number, since about half of our new members tend to disappear after about two years. Those who feel it is hard to gain a sense of belonging reported that they feel 'out of it' when people making announcements on Sunday mornings do not introduce themselves or wear a name tag. They feel disconnected when they see programs listed in the bulletin or newsletter but can't tell if those programs are something they should come to, and there is no name or number for them to call for further information.

"Oh, yes, we will lose one family fairly soon because they thought we were a Church of Christ, not a United Church of Christ, congregation. They moved up here from Norman, Oklahoma, and thought we had just merged—you know, "united"—two Church of Christ congregations. Needless to say, they have been really puzzled by a lot of things we do and don't do. But they were the only ones who have left because of significant theological differences. Mostly people who drop out say they have done so because a lot of little things weren't happening that might have made it easier for them to get on board. Other things include feeling really ill at ease during the coffee hour after worship. Some people feel uncomfortable with the small talk that coffee hours seem to require, and yet there aren't a lot of other times for people to meet new people at a significant level. For these people, the little molehills became big mountains. They said these little issues added up to a big message that they weren't welcome all that much."

Neal, chair of the evangelism and church growth committee, said, "That's why we asked you to do this new members feedback/reflection group. We will take this feedback and see what we can do to improve things."

Shelly said, "We will be meeting separately with the Christian education committee to talk about what we learned about the confirmation experience. That one is a bit of a puzzle, but we think we heard both the students and parents saying that the learning time is hampered by the behavior of some rowdy students. We also heard a request and a willingness for parents to show up and support the work of our ministers with this class. Some of the parents are pretty sure their kids will behave better if a parent or two are in the room."

"To close this year's report," said Shelly, "now that we have gone through our first year of feedback/reflection groups, we are putting together our plans for the next couple of years. Please let us know if you have a particular need for a group to provide feedback in the area of mission and ministry for which you are responsible."

The council continued that evening and for months afterward discussing the issues of music identified by the feedback/reflection groups. In the months that followed, the council also heard reports from the deacons and from the two pastors about the two new sermon study groups that had been organized. They heard from the evangelism and church growth committee the steps being taken to sensitize the whole congregation to what it is like to be a new member of Sand Lake Church. Feedback/reflection groups have become part of the life of this congregation. The groups have given members regular opportunities to complete the circle of healthy communication. And they are giving the ministers and other staff and the lay leaders of Sand Lake UCC regular, reliable, timely, humane, and proportional feedback about how their work is going.

LaVergne, TN USA
07 November 2010
203831LV00004B/8/P